The Preacher Calls an Audible

Dr. Joanne Nelson King Brown

VANTAGE PRESS
New York

Bible quotations are from the Living Bible copyright © 1971 and are used by permission of Tyndale House Publishers, Inc., Wheaton, Illinois 60189. All rights reserved.

Cover art by George Massey

FIRST EDITION

All rights reserved, including the right of reproduction in whole or in part in any form.

Copyright © 2004 by Dr. Joanne Nelson King Brown

Published by Vantage Press, Inc.
419 Park Ave. South, New York, NY 10016

Manufactured in the United States of America
ISBN: 0-533-14860-X

Library of Congress Catalog Card No.: 2004091371

0 9 8 7 6 5 4 3 2 1

To
John (Johnny) Downey King,

Truly a Man of God

Contents

Preface   vii
Acknowledgments   xi

1. Back in the States   1
2. The First Challenge   9
3. Off to Texas   16
4. The Pastor   22
5. Texas Vacations   30
6. A Live-in Mother-in-Law   34
7. Big City Woes   53
8. Time to Head West   65
9. This Mama Goes to Work   76
10. A Motorcycle Preacher?   84
11. Mexico Mission   89
12. After Mexico—Troubles   113
13. "Till Death Do Us Part"   120

Preface

The following are some of the titles I considered for this book:

Until Death Do Us Part (Life Is Good but Heaven Is Better)
or
There Is Life after the Mission Field (but Lots of Adjustments)

After a lot of pondering, I decided to use the title that John was going to use on the book he wanted to write some day.

This is my attempt to write a book about John, the preacher, and myself, as a preacher's wife, and our life after the mission field when he called audibles in the battle for his Lord, in order to help his team, the church, win Victory over the enemy of sin, indifference, and the devil himself.

When the quarterback gets to the line and sees how the defense is lined up he then may decide to change the game plan in order to have a better chance at defeating the opposing team. This is called "the quarterback calls an audible."

John came home from an especially long church board meeting one night, (the fact that sometimes only the spelling is different in the word "bored" should tell us something) and he declared, "I'm going to write a book and call it *The Preacher Calls an Audible.*"

He never stopped playing in his game of life long enough to write his book, so I am attempting to write it for him.

Most churches have a game plan. If it isn't working, the preacher needs to be brave enough to call an audible. Often audibles are necessary to counter the "We've always done it this way" approach—when God is perhaps wanting to move forward and meet needs in a new and relevant way.

I've noticed many times after the quarterback calls an audible, he gets knocked down, bruised, and yelled at, but gets up to continue the battle until he hears the final whistle. This is what happened to an Idaho cowboy turned preacher, who fought mightily for seven years beyond what was expected. He often came back to the bench (our home) so weak and weary, he felt he could not go out for another play, but then off he went into the thick of it, after talking with his coach (God Almighty). God left him in the battle (as a minister) for 26 years then took him to His home for eternity.

God knew others would be encouraged by the game he played, and the audibles he called while in the game of life.

I feel so privileged to have gotten to live with this man of God. May this book help you in your battle of life.

I have decided to make many of the names in this book fictitious, as some people did some mighty dumb things.

Acknowledgments

My gratitude goes to my present loving and understanding husband, Dale, for his advice, patience, encouragement, and love. He is mentioned only twice in this book. Once in the first paragraph, and alluded to in the last paragraph.

Thanks to all who helped me remember these seven years of ministry.

Thanks to our boys who have given me permission to "tell on them." They also were kind enough to share events and their feelings about those events with me so I could bring them to you.

Without a little 2-inch by 2-inch booklet my husband and boys gave me about "Football for Women," I would never have known about calling audibles. Thanks, fellas! Being the only female in a household of 5 and being the only one who had never played football, this booklet saved me from asking a bunch of stupid questions that no doubt would have been very annoying to my males engrossed in watching an exciting game.

1
Back in the States

A 49-year-old wife snuggled up to her kind, handsome, truck driver husband and his strong muscular arms wrapped lovingly around her, causing the events of the past to seem like another lifetime away. Her thoughts drifted back to 1968 when a Pan American airliner approached the Miami airport carrying a young missionary couple and their three small sons. All were weary from their long flight from Paraguay.

"Look, boys," the father beamed. "That's the good ol' U.S.A. down there!"

This was my family, and I was excited to see the U.S.A. again too. It had been four years since we had stood on U.S. soil and it would feel so good to be back home again.

We scrambled with the others to get

off the plane, still having hours of flying ahead of us but thankfully nothing like what we had just been through. I knew the next flight was not going to be pleasant. (John called it "the milk flight.") Up and down, up and down, stopping at every milk can along the way. That was his Idaho farm background coming out. That Idaho farm background was the reason we were back in the States two months before our furlough time was due. The cooking with lard plus six eggs, partially cooked bacon, biscuits and gravy, topped off with pie made with lard crust, *all for breakfast,* had caused cholesterol to clog John's arteries and now he desperately needed help.

He had confessed to me on the flight that he would like to be called "John" from now on, and not "Johnny." I had only known him as Johnny for the last fourteen years; this would take a little thinking on my part, but I found I could manage just fine.

In the airport John turned to me and whispered, "I'll take Timmy and Tommy, and you take Mickey, Angel, and we'll meet right back here." He had begun calling me "angel" years ago as he said I was his ministering spirit. It caused me to act the best I knew how. We each headed for our perspective bathrooms as fast as we could. We had bought the boys aqua cowboy hats so we could easily spot them in the crowded airports. Mickey laid his down on the floor in his stall and as quick as a wink, a lady next to him reached under and snatched it and ran out the door. Mickey began to cry. By the time I knew what had happened she was long gone. When we told John he replied sadly "Yep! We're back in the good ol' U.S.A. again!"

"Let's go get a real milk shake between flights. We haven't had real ice cream in years." John drooled, ushering us all toward the café counter.

"My homemade 'avocado' ice cream, made from powdered milk, left a little to be desired?" I suggested.

"Well, actually, a lot to be desired," he responded. He never was fond of avocados.

We all hopped up on the stools and soon were slurping down (way too fast) our most delicious chocolate shakes. While the fellas ordered another round of shakes I ordered celery, as I had really missed that. I just couldn't seem to get enough celery. In fact, it took years to fill me up on celery and I still enjoy it to this day.

Mickey was our adventurous one and he had no fear of running off. But in the crowds and confusion we lost him. Panic set in.

"We can't catch our next flight without him." John stated the obvious.

I ran to security and they took me to an office where a little blond boy sat happily eating an ice cream cone, wondering what all the fuss was about. After that, I could not relax until all three boys were tucked into their hotel room beds that night.

As I sank exhausted into the bed, it soon became apparent that the milk flight had really affected me. The bed would not hold still. I was landing the plane over and over again and bracing my feet for each landing. Mercifully sleep finally did take over.

Morning came way too early. Young boys do not believe in *sleeping in,* therefore young parents do not get that privilege either. This was the day we were to have our "debriefing" at our national office in Indianapolis, Indiana.

After the debriefing John turned to me and stated, "We're going to need a car so we might as well buy one here and drive out to our parents in the west."

I was to discover that preachers are not exempt from the fascination with cars. Knowing my lack of love for flying, he felt pretty secure that I would not object too much and he seized the moment. He was so clever!

Now, buying a car is a man's "thing" as far as I'm concerned. If it's a pretty blue it's OK with me. My only request was "<u>No Volkswagen bus,</u> like we had on the mission field, <u>PLEASE!</u> I have had enough of that type of vehicle to last me a lifetime." I thought I got my point across.

So, you guessed it—a Volkswagen bus is exactly what we got. At least it was blue.

As we traveled across country we discovered that our new vehicle could hardly make it up the hills. Everything passed us. The good thing was that it was nice and roomy so the boys could take naps when they got tired.

Often we would stop at a park with a watermelon in tow. John would whip out his trusty little pocketknife and lunch would be served. Then he would produce a ball and we all would play to stretch our legs and get exercise before we traveled on.

The boys were so good on the long trip out. The fact that every time they misbehaved their daddy would give them that "look," and I would take my foot off the gas pedal to let them know we could stop and help them think about their behavior, if necessary, certainly contributed to their being good little boys. John believed the Bible when it said "Spare the rod and spoil the child." The boys grew up very well behaved and thus were a joy to be around.

The boys didn't mind that I had to drive as my foot was heavy and the miles just slid by. John on the other hand never ever went over the speed limit. He felt that laws were to be obeyed and no cheating. He would often reprimand me for my heavy foot, but always in private, never in front of the boys.

We all wondered what our future would bring. John would have to find a job, as the mission field was no longer an option. He was not feeling good because of his heart condition and I wondered if he could work at all.

By the time we crossed the U.S. and made it to Eugene, Oregon, John was so ill we had to stop and stay in a motel for a few days until he could go on. I was anxious to get to my folks in Bellingham, Washington, which was just one day away; I knew I would have support there. Also our money was running very low and we would need to buy school supplies, shoes, and clothes for all three children. Mickey would start kindergarten, Tommy would be in second grade and Timmy would be a big fourth grader.

In a few days John was able to travel and we headed North to my folks' home. It was so good to see my parents again, and be on familiar soil! After driving over two thousand miles, I just collapsed! God hadn't given me more than I could bear, but it was close. What was to come next and where we would be going was still a mystery. I had to remind myself of the sign outside a church in England: "It doesn't matter where you live, as long as you live where you are."

2
The First Challenge

The next day we settled into a cheap motel and got the boys registered for school. The older boys adapted to school immediately but the teachers complained they had to get Mickey's older brothers to come translate for him. He was having a hard time with English. The boys spoke Spanish or Guarani (the Paraguayan Indian dialect) to each other whenever they could. This assured them others around them couldn't understand what they were saying. It proved to be a kind of secret society they had going for them.

The "cheap" motel came with a surprise! One morning in bed John whispered in my ear, "Something is biting me!"

I instantly jumped out of bed and cautiously pulled back the covers. I pulled a hair from where he said he was bitten then looked at it through a magnifying glass.

"Yikes!!! Something is crawling that has pinchers." I questioningly looked at John.

I had never seen "LICE" before but was soon to find out the misery of trying to get rid of them.

"Everything has to be washed in boiling water," my kind mother informed me. As I wasn't about to wash me or the kids in boiling water it didn't take me long to get to the drug store where we got some awful smelling stuff with which to wash ourselves. I was so grateful no one else but John played host to those critters. Just to be sure, I disinfected all our beds for fleas, too. What a way to start our time back in the States!

The first Sunday back at my folks, the conversation with the boys went something like this—

"No, you can't 'pee' in the neighbor's yard."

"Yes, you may play with the snakes but don't bring them in the house."

"No, you can't go to church without your shoes. Everyone here wears shoes."

"Yes, you're probably right, God doesn't care, but your mother does, so put them on, please."

The boys did eventually get civilized. We didn't have a TV for several years after we returned to the States, so they didn't have that to help or hinder their transition from jungle life to city life in America.

John wasted no time in getting to the public library to look up all they had on "cholesterol." It didn't take him long to find, in one of the books, the name of a medicine that was supposed to take your cholesterol down to that of a new born babe. After checking out the book he made an appointment with a doctor and, with book in hand he marched off to get the help he so desperately needed. Soon he had the magic prescription in hand. It turned out to be a thick, chalky, milky substance, but John gladly swallowed it down.

A few days later John ran out to me waving a letter that had just come. I was grateful for the distraction, as I was weeding Mom and Dad's garden—certainly not my favorite thing to do.

When I was a little girl in grade school, my sister and I used to weed what appeared to our young eyes as "mile long" rows of carrots or radishes. We would be paid the big amount of a penny a row; not real high wages even back then.

"There is a church in Grand Prairie, Texas, that wants to try a team ministry," John relayed to me with a grin and a hug.

"The minister there now is Bayne Driscall. He is getting older and wants a co-ministry with me."

Oh, he was so excited!

"I've never been to Texas before," I informed him. "Have you?"

"No, but that's OK."

Neither one of us knew they spoke another language called "Texan." We would manage, of course. I found a booklet that explained the new "Texas language" and how to pronounce various words. It would take a little studying. Many people had asked my mother if a Texas nanny had helped to raise me because of my way of speaking, so maybe it wouldn't be too hard.

An airplane ticket arrived in the mail shortly, for John. He was to go to Texas, to be interviewed and give a sermon. I knew I had better prepare to move to Texas, as John gave the most inspiring sermons I had ever heard, or ever hope to hear. But first, he needed a suit.

"This congregation has several millionaires in it, honey, so we better get me a nice suit!"

We had no money so we borrowed five dollars from my folks and headed for the Salvation Army thrift shop. John always was well built after our time on the mission field and handsome too, so the five-dollar suit looked like a million. If anyone was aware of its thrift shop background, we never knew. John pulled it off nicely (not the suit but the event with the suit). That became another in-house family joke, one you remind each other of and laugh about just before you fall asleep at night. We had a lot of those and there were a lot more to come.

Several days later I anxiously scanned the people at the huge Seattle airport for the handsome preacher I had sent off to Texas. He was such a good-looking man, in spite of the fact that his hair had long since left the front part of his forehead. Later, his young people would adorn his office with signs that read "Bald is beautiful" and "Bald is sexy." After awhile he also felt the need to get a wig, but seldom wore it (thank goodness). It looked so silly, like an animal was perched on his head ready to spring off at any time. As it got windy in Texas he feared it might blow off and that would be worse than no hair at all.

When our eyes finally met over a crowd of people and he winked I knew all had gone well. The man of God had shone through the five-dollar suit. John's humor, sincerity, and Christ-like Spirit came through loud and clear.

Mom and Dad had offered to keep the kids overnight so John and I could get a motel and have some private time to discuss our future. But the next morning as I was doing exercises with Jack Lalanne on TV and John was rolling on the bed with laughter, I wasn't so sure there was going to be a future if he didn't behave himself.

3
Off to Texas

"They want us to come right away, Angel." "That is OK with me; in fact, that is very good! We need the money and the kids need to get into their new schools." I assured John of my eagerness to go.

So, after saying good-bye to all our friends and relatives in Bellingham, we were off on another glorious 1,908 and 1/2 mile trip to our new home in Texas. On the way we stopped in Nampa, Idaho, to visit John's folks on their farm. The boys loved the farm! It would be the last time the boys and I would ever see Dad King alive, for soon after we arrived in Texas, Dad King's bad heart put him into the hospital. He told us he was just staying alive long enough to see his grandsons when they got back from the mission field.

John flew back to be with him and arrived in time to be by his side as he accepted Christ as his Savior. Dad King regretted so much that he had not done it earlier. John was elated. John had brought many to the Lord but this was the most meaningful for him, next to his own boys. We had prayed for Dad King for so many years.

When we pulled into Dallas, Texas, there were freeways going everywhere. The outside lane was always exiting unexpectedly so John stayed in one of the inner lanes, only to find that, as traffic joined us, another lane frequently came with them, thus putting us several lanes away from the exit instead of just one lane out. We were pulling a small U-Haul trailer, so we just couldn't pull in and out of traffic easily. John would find himself several lanes over from where he needed to be when it was time to get off. This just was not working; so the boys and I decided we had better try and help, in spite of the embarrassment it was causing John. We rolled down the windows, threw our arms out (this was before seat belts were invented) and pointed to where we needed to go.

Drivers laughed and motioned to let us in. As we breezed off at our proper exit I leaned over to John and said, "Everyone is so friendly!"

John cringed. "I hope no one in our new congregation saw us and will recognize us later," he moaned.

But of course, that was too much to hope for.

One of the parishioners in the congregation had a rental house they would let us stay in until we found a house of our own. We had no furniture—just dishes and pots and pans we had picked up at Goodwill. We had robbed my folk's fruit cellar of peaches and string beans to help tide us through until we received our first paycheck.

No one complained at all.

"Raising our boys in a third-world country where food is scarce does have its advantages," I confided to John after serving peaches and string beans for supper for the third night in a row.

"All the family has a different attitude toward *things* too. That certainly helps with the budget woes," John, smiling, chimed in.

After enrolling all three boys in school, and John meeting with Bayne to decide their individual duties, we began to feel settled. I walked the long halls of the huge church building and discovered that down one whole side were pictures of all the past preachers, and under their pictures were the dates of their ministerial service. None had stayed over two years and most had left after one year.

"I'm not even going to bother to unpack," I shared with John as I swung into his new office.

"I wonder if it is the hot summers or a hot congregation?" I questioned. Later I was to find out a different story on each one . . .

"As hot as it is in Texas, you wouldn't think that the Devil would stand a chance here," I confided to John. We were soon to find out that the Devil had a pretty good crew down there.

About the time I began to feel settled the church's co-pastor decided to move on and go into full-time evangelistic work. He was an exceptionally good evangelist. This left John with a congregation of a little under one thousand.

"I'd like to pastor it alone," he confided in me. "What do you think, Angel?"

"Not even a youth pastor?" I responded.

"Nope. I want to get to know our youth."

It seemed like a pretty tall order to me. Neither one of us knew that in four years John would be putting in eighty-hour weeks, week after week. This was in part because of five funerals a week, which required time spent in the hospital with the patient before death; time with the patient's family after the death, and five different sermons. (John never used the same sermon twice.) One Saturday night we didn't get home until four A.M. from the hospital after a death of a parishioner. It had been an eighty-hour week, and John fell into bed, crying.

"I don't have a sermon for tomorrow."

Now John believed one should spend one hour out of the pulpit in preparation for every minute in it. This just had not been possible. He felt that not to prepare was forcing God's hand—like Jesus being asked to jump off a high building and forcing the angels to catch Him.

He did fall asleep almost immediately and in the morning we prayed together for the Spirit to give him a message. He had been doing the Lord's work all week and I felt it was not *toooooo* presumptuous to ask for a message *word for word* from God.

Needless to say, that was the best sermon he ever preached! In spite of weariness he preached with power and conviction. At the altar call we had many come forward and rededicate themselves to the Lord, as John's words were so powerfully persuasive. It is an awesome experience to watch God at work through His Spirit.

4
The Pastor

Right after John accepted the position of "The" Pastor, we moved to a huge apartment complex closer to the church, and closer to all three boys' schools. We only had one car but John could walk to church and I could drive the boys wherever they needed to go, as well as run errands for John.

Good and evil things happened in the apartment complex. To go from the jungle to big city life was quite an adjustment. The first good thing occurred one morning after everyone had gone their separate ways. I was quietly having my daily devotions when the Lord seemed to be telling me to "Go to apartment 26C *now!*" I tried to reason it away but the urgent message kept repeating itself to me.

So, very timidly, I stepped out of my

safe haven and started to hunt for apartment 26C. It was not very far from our apartment so I found it much too soon for me.

As I raised my hand to timidly knock I heard sobbing inside. I told myself, "This must be the place."

A young lady in her twenties answered my knock. Her eyes were swollen from crying.

"Are you the one God sent?" she asked.

But before I could utter a word she continued, "Please do come in, come in!"

"I guess I am in, honey," I stammered as I followed her into the kitchen.

"I was praying to God to send someone!" I put my arms around the sobbing young woman and silently thanked God that He had pushed hard enough to get me to leave my safety zone.

We prayed together and I shared how much God loved her to the point of dying so she could have her sins forgiven. The morning sped by and I left her with the promise to return and invited her to come over to our house anytime.

I floated home. To be used by God gives one an indescribable inner joy. If I hadn't gone, I wondered whom the Lord would have picked to go. I would have missed out on such a blessing.

The church had a large kindergarten program and they needed a teacher.

"Why don't you teach, Angel?" John inquired one afternoon.

"That would solve our problem. You could be home before the boys came home from school."

"Because I can't get those easy puzzles together and night would fall and I would still be there trying to put the puzzles together." I teased.

"Why not just tell the children, 'No one leaves the room until all the puzzles are put away.'" Oh, he was so smart! Men do so love to solve your problems. So, of course, I accepted the position. That's when the awful reality of the big city hit me square between the eyes.

"We need to give you the 'troubled' ones, Joanne. We'll keep your classes small so you can handle them. Probably no more than ten or twelve at the most," the director told me.

"OK—but even twelve really troubled ones will be a lot," I responded doubtfully.

On my first day as I cheerfully bounced into my room, there sat twenty-three "troubled" children in front of me. One sweet small boy sat there wearing a very frilly little dress, with a bow in his hair. He told me his mother said she didn't want a boy, so he was not a boy but a little girl and she dressed him like one. He had to endure the teasing of his classmates.

He asked me, "Am I a boy or a girl?"

This is a great beginning for me, I mused.

Several kids had twitches and nervous blinking eyes. Their little bodies were reacting to the drama they had to endure at home. As the days passed I couldn't believe what my fellow teachers and the police were telling me about my precious little souls.

"Under no circumstances should Mildred be allowed to be picked up by her father," the director told me.

That same afternoon right after I dismissed my class and waved good-bye to them all, I heard gun shots ring out and I ran down the hall toward the back door and nearly ran into a policeman. The father had grabbed little Mildred and threw her into his car and sped off. The police had shot at him (but missed). He slowed the car, opened little Mildred's door and pushed her out. She was shaking, scratched, and black and blue, but thankfully no bones were broken. Her mother appeared just then and picked her up. How fortunate that one of the teachers had noticed Mildred's father cruising in the parking lot and she had called the police.

"What a fearful way to live! No wonder she had a twitch in her face. Who wouldn't have?" I lamented to John who had heard the shots too and had come downstairs from his office to see what was happening.

Bob didn't come to school one day, so

when I got a break I called his home to see if he was ill. There was no answer but the next day in the paper I found the reason. His mother was home taking a bath when two men came in and murdered her, leaving a note that said, "We got the wrong one but we'll get the right one next time." His mother had allowed another woman to live with them to help pay the rent. It cost her her life. Bob had come home from school and found his mother's body and had run to the neighbors for help. My little student, Bob, was taken to his grandmother's in another city.

As I was preparing supper one evening I heard the back door slam and soft footsteps coming toward me. A shy little Mickey was standing beside me looking dejected. One look at him told me he had done something that he shouldn't have. I noticed he was not wearing the new glasses that we had just recently bought for him.

"Where are your glasses, honey?" I inquired.

"I lost them when I was rolling down the hill," he lamented.

Well, there was nothing to do but gather up the family and go searching the hill.

"I don't need this aggravation," I complained to myself as I pushed tall thick grass to one side. The whole family, plus a friend or two, were on the hillside hunting for Mickey's brand new glasses. We really didn't have the money to get him a new pair so we desperately needed to find the pair he lost.

It was beginning to get dark and that's when the snakes come out. Knowing my fondness for snakes John was about to call the hunt off when it happened. As I reached my hand down to push some grass to one side I felt something slimy slithering away. Now we live between Fort Worth and Dallas and they tell me my scream reached the outskirts of both cities—plus shattering a few windows in the city of Grand Prairie, where the church was located. I personally don't believe it, but anything is possible.

"There will be no more hunting on this grassy hill tonight! That was a rattler, and pretty big, too. I'm sorry your mother had to be the one to find it," John informed everyone as he carried me out of the grass. Without me moving from my spot, I had jumped on his back the minute he had gotten close enough.

I knew it would not be easy to find the money for another pair of glasses, but we would just have to do it—so we did.

The first year slipped by so quickly and we were ready for a vacation.

5
Texas Vacations

Our vacations were usually tent affairs in June, coinciding with our wedding anniversary.

Thus, in order for me not to have to cook, the boys cooked and cleaned up. All I had to do was eat a boiled hot dog and have some cantaloupe for dessert. That proved to be a happy family memory, especially when we "dined" at the edge of the Grand Canyon. Any romantic notions that came our way were kinda dampened in a small tent with five of us breathing in each other's faces. John and I had a double sleeping bag that would have been nice on a cold night, but in July most anywhere in Texas is not a time for snuggling.

Not knowing the territory sometimes proved dangerous. One windy night (and it can get windy in Texas) we were having a hard time finding a place to pitch the tent. We all were very tired and hungry.

Finally John stopped and declared. "This is the spot! I can go no further."

I opened a can of soup while he tried to pitch the tent in the pitch dark. He secured it to the car with ropes. All night we both listened to the howling wind and wondered if our tent would stand up to the storm. The rains and hail soon followed.

As soon as daylight began to creep in the tent, John crept outside to look around.

"Oh, no!" I heard him moan.

I looked where he was pointing and felt faint. We were on the edge of a very steep cliff. I was so glad he had the forethought to tie the tent to the car, or we surely would have been in the bottom of the ravine. After that experience I thought nothing could shake me, but I was wrong.

One time, we were camping in the Ozarks, on a beautiful sunny day, the kind of day on which both man and beast like to sun themselves. Our three boys were having a lovely time running on the trails, hitting the big boulders with a stick as they ran by. All of a sudden shivers ran up and down my spine as John, walking behind me, yelled so loud the boulders could have shaken loose.

"Boys, drop your sticks and stop dead still. DO NOT MOVE!"

He rushed past me and grabbed the nearest boy in line and pulled him backward very quickly. Then I saw the problem. Good thing he took care of the situation, as this was something I could not deal with. Sunning itself on a big boulder was a huge rattler all curled up. The caretaker had heard John yell at the boys and came running with a machete. After taking one look at the snake, he went back for a bigger tool. He killed the snake and held it up for a picture. It was over six feet tall and had some beautiful rattlers.

The next day was Sunday and John took the boys hiking to the top of a small mountain nearby. I stayed and prepared lunch in camp. I could barely see them through my binoculars but made them out at the top. They were piling rocks and making an altar. There they worshiped

God, as their ancestors had done, centuries before. It was a moving experience for all.

6
A Live-in Mother-in-Law

After Bayne (John's co-minister) left, John had the responsibility of the church all by himself.

"It would be much better if you were to be with me when I go calling on the parishioners in their homes. Don't want any gossip to get started," he said with his crooked smile and a wink.

"Of course," I responded. And I gladly did just that.

I used to always go with John before we had the children. We knew of several ministers whose ministry had been ruined by tales of impropriety. But now we needed to have babysitters available in order for me to go with him.

Often he wanted me to go with him in the middle of the night when he was called out. This became a priority in our prayers.

Thus it came about that the Lord answered our prayers by providing a live-in babysitter (of sorts).

John's mother was a small, mousy looking woman who was made of steel. After Dad King died, she lived alone on the farm for a few months. One day we received a phone call from her neighbor saying she had been beaten up very badly and she was in the hospital. The neighbor would stay with her after she got home from the hospital until John arrived. After John hung up he looked at me with those puppy dog eyes and I knew what was coming. Of course we took her to live with us in Texas.

Our little apartment didn't have room for one more person so we started hunting for a house. Very quickly we found one not too far from the church. We moved in and John took off for Idaho to "fetch" his mother.

While he was gone I kept busy with the boys and making the house ready for one more person.

Protecting the boys in a big city, I was to find, was a full time job. Since we had left the States for the mission field and come back, times had changed.

One afternoon as I was walking to the neighbor's house (we had such wonderful neighbors) I noticed a car parked by the curb with a man in it. This did not seem right. I recognized him as one of the Dallas Cowboy football team. As we got closer I was horrified to see that as little children went by, he would expose himself to them. The boys and I turned around and headed back home.

"What a sick world we live in!" I told John that night in our daily phone call. I was so glad he would be home in a few days. The next day the newspaper ran a story about that player revealing that he had done this in several neighborhoods. I had to warn my boys about mentally sick people. I had had the privilege of growing up without fear and really wanted to give that legacy to my children, but it was not to be. The world had changed too much. Drugs had come onto the scene. I would have to talk to them about that too. Something I knew nothing about—but I educated myself quickly.

Years later a survey was done of the schools in our area and it came out that 98 percent of the kids had tried drugs of some sort. I sat my boys down and told them, "You boys better be in that 2 percent!" They assured me that they were.

How happy and relieved I was when that U-Haul from Idaho pulled up in our driveway! My hero had returned. His mother had barely stood the trip in the truck, what with all her bruises and aches and pains. She ate supper and went right to bed, which was the last time we would see her eat voluntarily. I think she wanted to starve herself to death. She was depressed. I had read that older people need plenty of water to keep their minds clear so I was always giving her water. It didn't help much.

Soon after we got her settled I knew that this would be an education in patience for us all. One evening after she had been with us for several months I complained to

John, "Honey, I've got to get away from her clicking false teeth."

I had already taken her to the dentist, who said there was nothing more he could do.

"Sure, Angel," he sympathetically agreed. "I know what you mean. I'll take you and the boys out to a drive-in theater and she can stay home and watch TV." Now that sounded wonderful to me.

As I started picking up the boys' jackets and headed for the car she asked John, "Where are you going?" The poor man didn't have the heart to leave her at home.

I read once that a young bride felt her husband thought more of his mother than of her and had asked him "If the three of us were in a boat at sea and your mother and I couldn't swim and the boat tipped over, who would you save?"

He answered, "My mother."

I thought this was awful but later changed my mind and thought the young bride better learn to swim. I knew how to swim and had to many a time. It didn't hurt me a bit and only served to cause my preacher man to love me more.

John's mother eagerly piled in the back seat. Once there, however, she began to complain (between clicks) that she couldn't see very well and could she come up in the front seat. She got out and somehow wiggled between John and me. I couldn't believe it! Now with three little boys in the back seat, not much would have gone on in the front seat anyway, but I had hoped for snuggling rights and a kiss or two . . .

John looked at me and winked, then smiled that crooked smile of his that always melted my heart. I was reassured, it told me "You're the best thing that ever happened to me."

Oh well—I did get to see the whole movie, except for when it was my turn to take the kids to the bathroom and for popcorn and drinks.

With three boys in school our finances were really stretched to the limit. Mom King didn't have any money coming in, as farmers back then didn't have Social Security. Her necessary medications began to eat up our paychecks and I was beginning to get concerned. Timmy needed a new mattress and there just wasn't any money for it. The Lord and I had a talk about this. I soon found out how He was going to solve the matter. The phone rang and one of the converts from San Diego, who now was a minister at Gresham, a church in East Texas, wanted me to come preach. I accepted.

The Saturday before I was to preach, I packed my clothes and our middle boy's clothes, and Tommy and I headed out for East Texas. I had no idea where I was going but had my antenna up to the Lord and I was listening to His voice. We had a wonderful trip. I was grateful for the time alone with the middle boy. Sometimes middle children feel left out. When we got to the town I hunted up a telephone and called the preacher's house. They gave me directions and we were able to find the parsonage easily.

They told me Jimmy Stewart's daughter would be in the congregation. He was one of my favorite movie stars. She was doing car commercials. I felt so privileged and hoped to see her.

The next day we woke early. As I was not a coffee drinker I could get right to work studying my sermon. I was excited about it, and eager to preach. Too soon it was time to go downstairs to breakfast. After breakfast and a nice visit, Tommy and I walked over to the church and I was happy to see him sitting right in front. I was nervous and it helped to see his smiling face.

The sermon went well and seemed to be so well received. It was with joy in my heart that after a nice lunch Tommy and I started home. The church was very generous and I had a check in my pocket to cover not only Timmy's mattress but some other needs as well. Tommy and I sang our thanks to our God all the way home. *God has given this lad such a beautiful voice,* I thought. As the years went by I discovered God had not played favorites as all three boys had wonderful voices, so easy to listen to.

A few days later old man winter had

set in with a vengeance. Snow was really coming down and the roads were slick and icy. John had left for work and I would be late if I didn't stop listening to Mom King, gather up my supplies and scoot out the door. We had two vehicles now, and mine got to stay in the garage so I didn't need to scrape the windows, or try to get a key in a frozen lock. I cautiously backed and slid down the driveway. The Lord and I kept a very active conversation going for the next two blocks as the curb and the car seemed to want to bump into each other. I wondered if I'd make it up the hill by the church. So many cars were wrecked there during ice storms.

I eased around my first corner and turned sideways. The car responded and I straightened it out. *This is kinda fun,* I thought. *But, I really don't want to get stuck and have to walk home in this storm so I better cool it.*

Just as I approached the bottom of that dreaded hill, I noticed several cars that had slid off the roadway into the ditch. Some had gone over an embankment and had tipped on their side. That didn't look fun.

Just as I was getting up my nerve to start up the hill I noticed a lone man standing by the road in the snow and wind. He was waving his arms at me.

Now who would want to ride with me? I asked myself.

It was John. *Oh, no! He must be stuck half way up the hill with all those other cars.*

I slid to a stop carefully as I didn't want to accidentally hit him. He stealthily hopped in the driver's seat, pushing me over. "Move over, Angel," he managed to get out through frozen lips. That was not a problem. I gratefully did so.

My Idaho cowboy turned preacher was used to driving on snow in Idaho. He just chugged right up the hill as if on dry pavement in the summer. We passed all the cars that were stuck and pulled into the church parking lot all safe and sound. There was John's car sitting there with no dents either.

The sacrifice he had made for me began to sink into my mind. He was the "angel" this time! He had braved the snow and cold windy storm, walking the mile to the bottom of the hill and around a dangerous corner to drive me safely to the top. His sacrifice meant more to me than any diamond necklace or any material gift ever could. His gift of loving kindness will last for eternity. It is true what the Bible says in 1 Peter 4:9: "Love makes up for many of your faults." I could never get mad at him after that as this incident would immediately flash into my mind. I never forgot his thoughtfulness and I asked the Lord to bring it to mind whenever I was tempted to become irritated with him. God certainly answered my prayer many a time.

    The boys loved the little Scottie dog the neighbors had. She shared with me how much each puppy would be worth. "Well, we certainly could never afford to buy one of those puppies," I confided to John.

    One day the neighbor came over and asked if we wanted to see her new puppies that had just arrived. We all trotted over. They were so cute!

"Which one would you like?" she asked me. That was not a hard question as one seemed to stand out so far above the rest. It seemed we had no choice; we were going to have to buy one whether we wanted to or not, so, as much of our budget would be going toward a dog, I picked the best of the litter.

"I'll bring it over to you as soon as they are weaned and have their shots."

Oh good, they would stand the expense of the shots! That would be helpful.

One day as John and I were trying to figure how to find the money to pay for the little Scottie, there came a knock on the back door. There stood the neighbor with my pick of the litter in her hand. I reached for the sweet little thing and John reached for the check book.

"Oh, no. We won't let you pay for this little fella. He is a gift to you and your boys. We know you will love him."

I felt very ashamed for picking the

best as I knew she could get top dollar for the one I chose.

"Please take this one back and give us a runt or one whose coloring isn't as pretty," I begged. "You could get a lot for this one! I am ashamed and I ask forgiveness for picking the best."

"We want you to have this one! So take it and enjoy him." Thus we received a pure-bred Scottie that was a true member of our family. We all loved him dearly, and he would be with us for many years to come. We decided to just call him "Scottie." This was a nice touch as John's ancestors were from Scotland and everyone felt he spoke with a brogue.

The boys were doing well in school and Timmy was doing very well in track and cross country. We tried to attend all his athletic meets. This proved to be difficult, but not impossible. There were times when life became very hectic, like the time Timmy had a track meet in East Texas, several hours away. John had a late afternoon wedding at the church in Grand Prairie. We watched our watches as the meet dragged on. Finally Tim's last race was due. All the contestants were ready. The gun went off once, and then again. Oh, no! Someone had started too soon. A false start and another delay as all the boys lined up again. The starter had the contestants get in position and then waited too long to shoot the gun. The boys' legs began to cramp in that semi-squatting position which should never have been held so long. A second false start—and time was ticking away, but John was determined to see his boy run. It seemed forever before the gun went off again.

Finally there was a clean start and the runners were off. Tim was in front and we yelled and yelled. I became hoarse and hoped John's voice held out. We hugged each other as Tim crossed the finish line first. It seemed impossible to make it back to the church in time.

"You drive, Angel, and I'll change my clothes as we go," John yelled at me as we ran across the parking lot to the car. He knew I drove faster than he did but we both knew he was going to be late.

"I told the groom not to go into the sanctuary until I arrived. He knows we were coming from East Texas. I hope he will wait."

He started stripping off clothes in the front seat of the car. When he got down to his shorts I looked at him and said, "Let's hope we don't have a wreck or I get pulled over for speeding by a lady cop!"

As our car was not big and John was, it made it very difficult and funny. I finally stopped and let him in the back seat so he would have more room to maneuver. Off I sped again as precious time clicked by.

The time for the wedding came and we had just arrived in town. I pulled up quickly to the church front door and let him out. He looked pretty good for dressing in a small car. He would be wearing his clerical robe anyway. That would help.

Afterward he told me the groom had not waited and was standing there in front. "I laughingly told them, 'You'll have something to share with your kids someday,' " he said, feeling a little bit guilty for being late.

John and I tried also to watch all Timmy's football games. I was told never, no matter what happened, never, *never,* to go out on the field. If Timmy got hurt and his daddy felt it was serious enough, he, and he alone could go down—but under no circumstances was I to get out of my seat. I obeyed this unwritten rule even though it was very hard at times.

The Texas sun was blazing down on us in the stands, one fall afternoon, as we were watching a very important game. The ball was heading straight for Timmy. I held my breath and prayed. I could have saved my efforts, as afterward he related what happened.

"I asked the Lord 'could I please make a touchdown?!' Then I looked up and saw the ball coming right at me. I knew it was my answer to prayer and the Lord was telling me 'YES,' so I caught it. But just as I caught it I was tackled. Now, I knew that God didn't give me that ball *not* to make a touchdown so I spun around and shook the tackler off and began to run with all my might toward the goal line. I didn't even look behind me, I just ran! I was so grateful when I crossed the goal line and immediately began to thank the Lord for His answer to my prayer."

I too thanked the Lord, not for Timmy's touchdown, but for revealing Himself to my boy so he would have a very personal relationship with Him. You cannot give your children your faith but when they demonstrate their own faith, words cannot describe the pleasure it gives to you.

There was one boy on the football field each week. I noticed that he never had a daddy in the stands for him. No one to cheer him on, or tell him how well he played. I asked one of the mothers next to me about it.

"That's the Macabee boy. His daddy was murdered just six months ago. They found his body in the trunk of his car. They still don't know who did it."

You never know when you look at someone what burdens they carry, do you? I asked John that evening as I related what the mother had told me.

"Then there are some burdens that are very obvious, like Tommy's friend, Rusty." John reminded me.

Rusty was a joy to have around. We all just loved him. Rusty had had polio as a very young child and it left him with one arm and hand all shriveled up and useless. He also had really bad allergies. He could not tolerate milk. When he stayed with us and we had cold cereal for breakfast (or snack time, anytime), he would just cheerfully put orange juice on his cold cereal as if that was the most natural thing. Rusty was such an inspiration to us all, especially when we were playing basketball in the backyard. Rusty also had a growth problem and was very short for his age, so one would not expect him to excel in basketball. Rusty threw his whole self into whatever he was doing, often getting hurt in the process, but it never slowed him down one bit. If you could beat him in basketball you really had to earn it. He was good. Thank you, Rusty, for the life lessons you taught us. I can still hear your laughter.

7
Big City Woes

A few days later John and I were sitting in his study at church discussing the dangers we were facing with our boys here in the big city. "What was that?" I gasped to John. "It sounds like gunshots!"

We ran out the front door in time to see a car speeding away from a parked car just 1/2 block from us. A woman got out of the car screaming. I ran on over to her while John ran back into the church and called the police.

She told me, "My husband pulled in front of that other car and it made the driver mad. The other car then pulled up to us and forced us off the road. He yelled some things, drew out his gun and shot my husband several times." She was shaking and sobbing. John stayed with her until the police came.

The corner store near us displayed pornographic magazines right out in plain view. We had just heard on the news that a rapist had blamed porno magazines for the fact that he had raped. John decided to do something about it. He brought the matter up at the next city ministerial meeting, and also at the church elders meeting. Both groups went down to the magazine store to talk with the manager and owner about the situation. John had such a persuasive way about him I knew something would get done, and it did. The owner said he would put the magazines behind the counter if John would tell him which ones.

The news media got hold of the story and arrived at the store at the same time as the ministers who had come to help John select which magazines were the worst offenders. John spoke with them at length.

"I could not believe my eyes, Angel," he lamented to me that night. "Some of it was so bad. It ought to be against the law to publish that stuff."

Now I was like the soldier boy whose

grandma was so worried about her grandson that she asked at the first opportunity, "Do they have pornography in the service?" To which the boy replied, "Why, shucks grandma, we don't even have a phonograph." I really was not sure just what John was talking about and I really didn't want to know.

John took some of the magazines to the next elder meeting at church. The men were shocked and lined up behind him 100 percent. The paper came out with John's picture on the front page captioned "Local pastor going through the porn magazines."

To offset the evil around us we gave our boys every opportunity to know and experience Christ's way. John was a loving but very strict papa. When the boys would complain he would tell them, "I am raising my sons for the Lord, not entering a popularity contest." They knew it was useless to say more.

At church I tried to be the disciplinarian, pinching them quietly if they acted up in church. As soon as they got big enough to sit with their friends at church, they always asked to do so. One time, shortly after we had arrived in our new church, the middle boy was having a bad day and began to make a fuss. It got to the point where he was disturbing others during his Daddy's sermon. John had tried "the look" but Tom wouldn't look at him. The next thing we knew, John was saying from the pulpit, "Excuse me for just one moment, please."

In shock Tom saw his father approaching him with "that look." John grabbed Tom's sleeve and propelled him out into the hall via the nearest door. Our other two boys just looked at me, horrified. Soon John returned with a very repentant little son whose eyes were showing signs of tears. John marched back to the pulpit and continued his message. He had the rapt attention of at least one person in the sanctuary that morning.

"Can you believe that some of these people feel if your skin is dark you are inferior in some way? I've got to do something to help," John lamented to me.

I knew he was cooking up something that could be very dangerous here in the South. There were people in our congregation who had owned slaves and still had the same families but they were paid a wage now for their labor. The little song we used to sing as kids, "red and yellow, black and white, they are precious in His sight" was just a given for me. It never occurred to me that anyone was in any way "lower" than I, nor "better" than I. It just was not a problem; the way you conducted yourself determined what kind of a person you were, not how dark or light your skin was, nor if you were blond or redheaded. (I just had to throw that last part in, due to so many blond jokes going around, and the feeling that redheads have tempers.)

John asked a very famous black preacher from Dallas, who had preached at one of our national conventions, if he would come preach at our church. We felt humble and excited when he agreed to do it. But the only time he had open in his very busy schedule was a Sunday night.

"Please put us in the one empty spot,"

John pleaded. John had explained the situation and the attitude of some of our folk.

"Don't worry, brother," the black preacher said. "I am used to it." *What a crime for a man of God to be treated so badly,* I thought.

Word got out that a black man was coming to our church. One of the vocal elders of the church came to John and declared, "If he steps foot in this church I will ask him to leave and I will hand in my resignation."

John, kindly as could be, said calmly and sweetly—but firmly, "We will hate to see you go."

The appointed night came and we wondered if anyone would show up. To our surprise the lower part of the sanctuary was packed. "We might have to use the balcony!" John whispered.

Then in marched that particular elder. I sucked in my breath as he walked deliberately to the front of the sanctuary and sat down in front of the pulpit.

"What if he should hop up and start

shouting at our famous speaker?" I fearfully asked John.

"Trust God. Hearts will be changed tonight." And they were.

After the service that elder went up and shook the speaker's hand, then told John. "I'm glad I came tonight." Nothing was ever said again about his handing in his resignation. Durinig the weeks that followed, many people came up and confessed to John their initial prejudice and how "that wonderful speaker" had changed their minds.

That same elder gave John grief some time later when the son of one of the millionaires in the church, who had gone the drug and hippie "way out" route began teaching the high school class at church. John firmly told him to go sit in his class for a few Sundays, then come back "and we'll talk." John knew the lad had met the Lord in a mighty encounter on a mountain in Montana. He gave his life to the One who had died for him and now was telling everyone about his Jesus. He studied his Bible daily. Well, "that elder" did go sit in on the class and came out telling everyone what a wonderful teacher the high school class had. He was the young man's biggest fan.

I am so glad my husband never backed down just because the devil came calling. John always stood up for God's people, even if it was risky.

Speaking of risky, there were snakes in Texas too. Tim, the eldest, delighted in killing water moccasins, bringing them home, skinning them and putting them on a board to dry. Knowing my lack of fondness for snakes he would hide the corpses where he thought I would not find them, in the lawn mower shed. Having three boys I never had to mow the lawn. One day I did have to go into that shed and all the neighbors up and down the block soon knew that I had done so. My screaming did not cause alarm, as it seems everyone knew about the snakes in the shed but me. They were all just waiting to see what would happen when I accidentally found them. That seemed a bit too dangerous for my small lads to be doing, so I asked them not to do that anymore.

"But Mom," Tim responded. "I swim with them at Boy Scout camp all the time!" This was certainly a shocker to me.

This was not the jungle but Texas seemed to have its share of poisonous things. When the janitor at the church moved away and we were without someone to clean weekly, John enrolled his family temporarily. Now I had heard of scorpions, with that curly tail sticking up. I knew they were poisonous and could kill old people and small children, plus make anyone else very sick indeed.

When my youngest son, Mickey, was sweeping the floor ahead of me, while I mopped it, he yelled, "Oh, look at that cute little bug, Mamma!"

"Don't touch it," I screamed, hoping to get John's attention. Failing to do so I figured the killing of this creature was going to be left to me. John always swatted the flies just to the right of them, missing every time so maybe it was best I stomp on this one. I was just wearing my beach flip-flops and my whole foot was exposed, so I knew I had better get it right the first time. I wanted to close my eyes but I figured that might not be too wise.

Just then the scorpion decided it had stayed in that spot long enough and darted along the baseboard. It was heading straight for my middle boy, Tom. Now I knew I would have to take off my shoe and put my hand in the flip-flop to smash it. Quick as a flash my shoe came off, my hand went in it and there was one dead scorpion. When the boys told their dad he didn't believe it.

"I've got to see that scorpion," he laughed. He stopped laughing when the boys led him to the dead curly-tailed thing against the baseboard. "We've got one brave mother, don't we, boys?" he said as he led us all to the car. "This calls for a taco all around."

"Yeah! Yeah!" the boys shouted their approval as we drove to our favorite church member's taco stand on Main Street. We always tried to pay him but he never ever took any money. That was a kind deed as it allowed us to eat out once in a while in spite of our money crunch.

After church one day, a widow lady came up to John and said, "Pastor, I'd like to give you something. You have helped me guide my two children successfully through high school and I am so grateful."

John was very flattered.

"Would you please go to this address and speak with this man? He will do the rest. I have made all the arrangements."

John was so excited; the card she handed him was that of a tailor in Dallas. John had never had a suit made just for him! Maybe she was tired of his five-dollar suit. We eagerly went to Dallas that next day and hunted up the address.

"So many different kinds of materials, so many styles of suits," John whispered to me. "Help me! Please."

It was fun. They took all the measurements and then we had to go home and wait. That was the hard part. Finally the call came and we rushed over to pick up the suit.

Wow! Was John ever good-looking in

his tailor-made suit. (That suit would last him 'til the Lord called him home.) Many a sermon was preached in that suit, many a wedding (or funeral service) performed. What a thoughtful and helpful gift! We all do our best when we think we look good. It makes it easier to think of others when you can forget about yourself.

Making calls on his parishioners was one of John's best traits. We called on saint and sinner, well and sick, day and night. All it took was a phone call. I usually went with him at night, as going on the wet highway at night took more than one pair of eyes. Some of our best fellowship was at two or three in the morning, coming back from a hospital call or a jail call. The rewards more than made up for the lack of sleep.

8
Time to Head West

By 1972, the eighty-hour weeks, the strain of John's mother living with us, the boys doing so well in sports, and John's desire to go back to the Northwest all combined to convince him to send his resume to the District Minister of Oregon to see if a church was available.

"I hope there is a church in Eugene, Oregon, so Tim would be able to continue his running. He is so good at it." (Eugene was considered the running capital of the State.)

I eagerly went for the mail each day. Finally a letter came from the Northwest Minister. There was a church open in Penelton, Oregon. John would not even consider it. No track program good enough for Tim and all the meets would be too far away for John to attend, and attend he intended to do.

A few weeks later another letter came, the church in Springfield, Oregon, had an opening. That was just perfect. We got a plane and both of us got to go out for the interview. I nearly blew it! When, in a very serious meeting with the congregation, one of the men asked me "And what do you do?"

Without thinking, I replied, "I go to the church down the street."

John laughed and then so did everyone else except that gentleman. Knowing John's policy of only going to a church if the vote was unanimous, I feared that gentleman might cast the one "no" vote. But I needn't have worried, as John's sermon was so powerful it more than made up for his mouthy wife.

On the flight back we discussed what to do with John's mother. We had looked at houses big enough to keep her but she was getting to a place where she needed to go into a care home. In the end she solved the problem. She wanted to go to a home in Idaho for Rebeccas (she had risen in rank in the organization and really liked it and many of her friends were there). We could drop her off on our way to Springfield.

The call to come to Springfield came the next week, and John handed in his resignation. (At least the dates under his picture were longer than any so far in the long hall of past ministers.)

It was a very hot day when John pulled up in the driveway with the U-Haul truck. My folks had flown down to help us move and now were both sweating profusely. Mom and I finished scrubbing the kitchen (some places in corners with a toothbrush) just as the fellas finished loading the truck.

We had bought an airplane dog carrier for Scottie and after saying our good-byes to him we packed him over to the neighbors, who would put him on the plane when we arrived in Springfield, Oregon.

We headed out. The plan was to keep each other in sight and avoid all tornadoes. It was the season for the rascals and I really didn't want to see any more of them in my lifetime. We had not gone far when I looked at Mom and her face was red as a beet. She could not handle the heat and we had no air conditioner in our car. She could have a heat stroke! I turned off the main highway and hunted for a grocery store that I knew would have air conditioning.

Soon after Mother got into the store she was better. We waited awhile until her face went back to normal, then headed out again. I knew we had lost the fellas and we were not too keen on driving all the way by ourselves. I didn't even know where we planned to spend the night. There was no way to communicate with them.

What a beautiful welcome sight came upon our eyes as we left town. There, on the side of the road, was the U-Haul.

"Oh, no! They have broken down already!" I lamented. But of course that was not the case at all. They were just waiting for us. I don't know who was happier to see whom. Soon we were off again. We would take coffee breaks, meal breaks, and bathroom breaks. We missed very few rest areas on the way, changing drivers and passengers every few hours. Still the trip back seemed to take forever.

As we came to a certain spot where the road came very close to a hill the boys delighted in recalling a very embarrassing time on a bus trip out to California. It was a rare time when it was just the boys and I. We were traveling via Greyhound Bus and having a grand time. All of a sudden, I felt the need to sneeze! Now you must understand that I had inherited how to sneeze from my father, who had inherited it from his father and who knows how far back it really went; a very, very loud sneeze. So as I let loose with the family sneeze, Timmy ran to the front of the bus, cupped his hands over his mouth as if to make a megaphone and yelled at the top of his voice, "Take cover! There's going to be a landslide."

A few days later our moving procession was finally crossing the Cascade Mountains. Upon entering the beautiful, lush green Willamette Valley one's eyes could barely take it all in. The tall stately green fir trees swaying gently in the breeze; a beautiful bald eagle swooping down into the valley of trees below. Flying low over a roadside crystal lake, an eagle had caught up in his talons a big trout. "His little ones will eat good tonight," I remarked. A smile blossomed on my face and has never left. This valley would cradle my family for years and years to come. Sports here would be good to all three boys.

Tired and exhausted, we found a Motel 6 and ended our road trip in Springfield, Oregon. We all gave thanks to God for our safe journey.

The next day was sightseeing day, great fun. We would stay in the motel for awhile until we could find some place else to move to. We would have to store our things for now. We said our thank yous and farewells to my folks as they boarded the bus for Washington State.

"The first order of business better be to find a house to move into," I pleaded with John. "The motel is OK but no place to keep little boys for very long." We all missed our dog and couldn't send for him until we had a place for him to stay. One of the church families offered us their home to stay in while we hunted for our new home.

When John and I started out in the ministry, all churches had parsonages. Now it was very common for the preacher to buy his home. John, of course, wanted one within walking distance from the church. This might be a tall order for us humans—but not for God. It seems there were some new houses being built just up the street from the church. One of them even had four bedrooms!

"What a blessing four bedrooms would be," I confided to John. "Each boy could have his own room."

John, ever cautious, said, "We will have to see what we can borrow from our national board."

The house we were looking at would have church members all around us, and this would prove to be oh so nice when tragedy struck.

After what seemed like forever we finally heard that we were approved for the house loan. It wasn't long before our furniture was coming in the door and I was directing traffic as to where to put things. This would be the first time John actually would not have an office in the house as well as at the church since San Diego. He would always try to throw his day's load and work at the bush by the front door before he entered. For this we were all to benefit. I expected the bush to die very soon, but, alas, it outlived him.

The first order of business was to put up a fence and send for Scottie. We all pitched in and got the fence up in record time. Next thing we knew we were on the way to the airport. I wondered if Scottie would remember us or be mad at us for leaving him and making him fly out. I needn't have worried for he was delighted to see us, but once out of the carrying crate he never would enter it again, or even go near it. He had had enough of that. His love of flying must have equaled mine. It was so good for us all to be back together again! Scottie seemed to love his new yard and ran around and played ball with the boys.

Soon after we arrived John received a frantic call at the church from a woman whose niece was dying of cancer. She wanted John to come to her house and pray for healing for the young woman. John called me and asked if I would go with him. He never went to a home where there was a woman alone, regardless of her age, without me or one of the elders going with him. It is so sad but many an innocent pastor has had his ministry ruined by a spurned woman wanting revenge.

"Sure, honey, just let me get out of my shorts and into some slacks. How about five minutes?" I responded. I felt privileged to share his ministry.

I was waiting out front when he pulled up and we were off. An elder joined us there. As we entered the living room where the young lady was lying in a hospital bed, I could smell death. Now I had seen people healed and been in on the circle of prayer but also had fear of a "No" answer causing lack of faith in the woman who had requested the prayer. I myself could not always understand the why of a "No" answer. Had I not fasted and prayed and pleaded with God for the healing of a little eight-year old girl in Texas and then she died? Why? This would be the first call for healing here in Springfield and how would a "No" answer affect our ministry here?

John always explained before we prayed that we had no power whatsoever to heal, only God could do that. We were but His instruments should He choose to use us. We did not beg or plead or "tell God what to do." We simply opened ourselves to Him for His use.

As we gathered around the young woman and put our hands gently on her I began to feel that something mighty was going to happen.

"Will you lead us in prayer, Joanne?" he nodded my way. I began to talk with God and as I talked I felt heat going through my arm into the young woman. The heat became more intense. I knew God was working and I began to relax and smile. Joy just sprang up within me. We sang a hymn and reverently left. When we

reached the car I asked J⎵
that heat?"
"Oh, yes. Wasn't that so⎵
humans have so much to learn⎵
ways. We think we can tell Him ⎵   ⎵
his business but He lets us know⎵ ⎵ His
business and He knows a little more about
it than we do. We like to put God in a box
and we don't like it when He does things
we don't expect or understand and doesn't
fit our idea of Him."

We learned later that week that the young woman went back to her doctor and they found that her cancer had dried up and she was cancer free. Neither one of us were surprised. The word really spread and our healing ministry was so blessed in Springfield. God did mighty wonders there.

John sought out the Full Gospel Men's Fellowship group in Eugene. Their meetings were so helpful to us. They renewed our faith. This group inspired us so much in Texas.

9
This Mama Goes to Work

Although John had years of schooling and graduate work, and was working on his doctorate, the salary in the ministry did not begin to compare with others with like education and years of experience. Therefore as our bills piled up, I discussed with John the idea of me taking a job. He seemed open to it so I became excited when reading the classified section the next day and ran across an ad that said, "Cashier type wanted."

Now if anyone was a cashier type, it was I. Little did I guess the paper had left out a comma after the word *cashier*. So I jotted down the address, and the next day found me interviewing for the *cashier type job*. It was for an optical shop. That job would change my life forever.

I had a rude awakening when the boss

asked me to type something up for him. I had taught typing in South America but only by the book. I didn't really know how to type. The boss didn't realize the paper had left out the comma after "cashier" so I was in a pickle. I sat down at the typewriter and was giving it my best shot when my immediate boss came in and heard and saw my efforts.

"You can't type, can you?" he asked.

"Not very well," I honestly replied.

"Well, I used to be a recorder in the navy and I know how to type. I will help you." He sat down and had it all typed up in no time. I was never asked to type again.

One day as I was counting out the money to start the day I could not make it come out right as it had the night before. I was getting frustrated.

Finally my fellow employees told me, "Don't worry about it! The big boss takes money from the till and doesn't put in a note. He wants to see if you are honest and doing your job."

This made me very angry, as much time had been spent trying to figure out what was wrong. I called the boss up, explained what happened and asked him to please leave me a note in the future if he ever took money from the till again. He obliged me from then on.

After about a year my immediate boss started his own shop and I went over to work for him. He and his wife were Baptists from Texas and that was a good combination. We worked well together. Later they asked John to be the preacher at their son's wedding.

As John became well known in the community, his counseling load increased to the point he had to limit it or give up time for his own family. His philosophy was "God gave *me* three sons to raise. If I don't do it, who will?"

John never neglected his own sons for other people's children. He'd say, "Too many preacher's kids grow up hating the church, cause Dad's never there for them."

John would tell the boys, "If you threw eggs on someone's porch, we'd clean it up together no matter how embarrassing it would be for me." They knew he meant it and they lived accordingly. We told our boys, "You must act beyond reproach not because you are a preacher's kid, but because you are the child of the KING." They knew we meant the child of the King of Kings—not just their earthly name King.

He made time for sporting events the boys participated in and time to check up on them. Like one time Tim had been told he could not go to visit his girlfriend but he grabbed his bike and determinedly headed out the driveway. As he told his brother later, "I was heading for Traci's house and happened to turn a corner and looked back. There was Dad in the car following me. I made a U-turn and Dad smiled and waved and drove on."

Another time, John was not real happy over circumstances which came later that year.

"Mom, Dad, I just got a letter saying my girlfriend from Texas is coming in on an airplane next week. What shall I do?" Tim questioned us. Now Tim was only in junior high. Kid's don't usually have girls flying over the country to see them at that tender age. But she was coming. Now she was a nice girl but Tim had made new friends and this could be very embarrassing. Tim would have to move in with one of his brothers and give her his room. We would have to plan what we would want to do while she was here. No doubt drive over to the ocean and up to the mountain where she could throw a snowball or two.

John laid down some rules for family behavior while she was with us. One important rule was "The bedroom door is never to be shut when the two of you are in there." It wasn't long before that rule was broken. John strode down the hall and opened the door with a jerk. Then he said—more for the guest's benefit than for Tim's—"This door is to remain open. Am I understood?"

It was never shut again to my knowledge while she was there, or later when any other girl came to visit.

When we put her on the plane it was a relief for all of us. On the way back from the airport we sang a song that was popular then, "Leaving on a Jet plane; Don't know when I'll be back again." Our humor was not appreciated by Tim, but it was a bonding family experience anyway.

Tim's friend was not the only visitor we had from Texas. If you are a millionaire and your marriage is in trouble it is certainly worth it to fly across the country to get counseling from someone you trust. John was very good at helping couples see how they could improve their marriage. His reputation followed him. John would not charge the couple, he told them, if they did exactly what he told them. But if they didn't, then he would expect to be paid by the hour and his fee was very, very high. He never had to be paid by the hour, and he saved many a marriage. The couple that flew up from Texas he took on, but told them he couldn't accept others from Texas as he owed it to his present congregation not to get overloaded.

The night after the couple arrived John asked me, "Angel, will you take the wife for a walk by the river tomorrow and counsel her while I talk with the husband?"

Now I knew the best counseling is listening and I felt I could do that just fine, so off we started the next day, she and I. She did have a lot to spill and get out of her system. I also knew the helpful thing to say is "Now, what do you think about that?" That night John and I compared notes and he took it from there. They stayed two weeks and headed back to Texas. We heard from them each Christmas until John's death. Their marriage grew stronger and stronger. We were so happy for them.

"You know, what bothers me about marriage counseling is that the women complain about the same things you do," he confided to me one day.

I attributed our happy marriage to his counseling other couples and then coming home and saying, "Do you feel like that?"

John had to limit his counseling so he could do the calling on his people that was requested both at their homes and in the hospitals.

"Let's go to the mountains and play today," John suggested one day when the boys were out of school. I quickly boiled some eggs but didn't want to take time to devil them so took them with shell and all; then threw some more food in for an impromptu picnic and we were off. When we came to a nice picnic spot we all piled out of the car. The fellas played in the snow while I put the food out. It was cold but I just peeled those eggs with my gloves on. John ran and got the camera but had trouble holding it still enough to take a good picture because of his laughter.

We had just made another memory that you laugh at just before you fall asleep at night. Our album of those kinds of memories was getting very thick, and we would soon be needing to open it and peek inside.

10
A Motorcycle Preacher?

Preachers on motorcycles in Springfield, Oregon, were not a common sight. But as motorcycles needed far less gas than any auto at that time it was essential to consider their advantages once again. At least this time there would be no ruts, fallen logs or creeks to be traversed, as in South America. However, we did not count on the rudeness of cars and the stupidity of some car drivers! At a stop light they would come up and almost hit your back bumper. When "my bumper" was sitting on the cycle's bumper, I did not appreciate this. So, finally, John mentioned in the pulpit about the discourtesy of some drivers. Word got around and we had far less trouble after that. I dare say many another cyclist could thank us, too.

    John made quite a stir at the hospitals, both in Eugene and Springfield, when he would walk down the hall in his suit and tie, carrying his helmet and jumpsuit. "Everyone treats you differently when you have a helmet under your arm!" he used to complain.

When John went to the courthouse to lend support to a family whose child was being sentenced for drug use, a felony which seemed to be coming up way too often, it was much easier to find a parking place if we had the motorcycle than if we had the car.

One of the sad parts of the ministry is seeing one of God's young, beautiful creatures burn or fry their brains with drugs. Often the parents were the last to know. Maybe because they didn't want to know; surely the signs were there. As John was friendly with the police they would not hesitate to call him when one of our church members would request him to come down to the jail and talk with them. One particularly beautiful young woman asked John to come down to the police station so she could tell him her story. He asked me to come too. Her trial was to be held the next day.

Her story was that she was at a party and was in the kitchen when the police came and raided the party. Drugs were found in her apron pocket; she claimed someone must have slipped them in there and she did not notice.

She was scared.

The next day John and I sat through the proceedings with butterflies in our tummies. What would happen to this young woman? It must grieve God when sin gets such a grip on His children! She was not spared; we learned this was not her first time. She had no parents in the court room to hug her or to cry with her at the sentencing.

Within a week John was parking his cycle again at the court house, this time to be with a young man accused of selling and using drugs. The court assigned him probation and gave him over to John to watch. John did not feel good about the outcome of this situation. The parents were in denial that their son could do anything wrong, and "if" he did, it was always someone else's fault.

Late one night we were coming home from church. It was still light enough to see but eerie dusk time. We passed a house and I saw John's charge in a yard, putting a package behind a bush. John slammed on the brakes, hopped out of the car and ran to the bush. Sure enough it was drugs. When we got home he called the lad and asked him to meet him at the church.

A very defiant young man marched into John's office later that evening and declared, "That package you found under the bush wasn't mine!"

John laughed and replied, "How did you know I found a package?" He knew it would do the lad no good to let him get away with it.

John felt very strongly that the parents of wayward young people needed to face facts and realize they must have a part in the recovery of their offspring. He would mince no words in letting them know their life would influence that of their child, telling the parents that God was the only answer strong enough to whip their problem. If they loved their child, they would have to get to know God through His son, Jesus and His word, the Bible. When John left the parents knew he meant business and he expected them to be in church the next Sunday and every Sunday after that. I personally do not know of any parent that he spoke with who did not come to church and get to know God, and in many cases the young people came too (when they got out of jail).

11
Mexico Mission

"The old school bus looks pretty good all painted up," John smiled at me. "I hope it runs and stays in one piece until we get back!"

We had just passed the church on our way to the hospital for one last call before we headed to Mexico with the young people on a mission.

"We still are lacking some funds. Angel, how can you possibly feed all of those who are going with the money we have raised and still be able to pay for gas? I am worried."

"Don't you be concerned, Tiger. Remember, the Lord fed 5,000—what's a mere thirty-four people?" I reminded him.

We both knew how hard the young people had worked to raise money for this trip. Among other projects, we sponsored a

"Lock-In-Rock-In." Everyone found sponsors to sign up for so much money for every hour they rocked in a rocking chair. We got a lot of rockers and had them brought to the church. We furnished snacks and they got a break every fifteen minutes to stand, walk or whatever for five minutes. They sang, played games and kept each other awake. By morning, everyone was ready for his or her own bed! Some of the young people baby-sat to earn money; they also cooked spaghetti dinners for the church family. They had all earned points by doing various Christian projects, plus reading and memorizing the Bible. We were so proud of each one of them.

As we sped along on the motorcycle I began to pray. How would God "fix" our problem? It was going to be exciting. I began to sing (or rather hum, as one does not sing on a motorcycle). I hummed a song we used to sing in college. "Nothing, nothing, nothing is impossible with God."

The man we were going to call on had not accepted Christ (yet). He had just had a hip replacement; he was a logger and a pile of logs had rolled on him. The impact would have killed most men, but this was a huge, tall, strong Paul Bunyon type, not easy to kill. I knew God loved this man as I did, for his kind heart. In spite of his rough exterior, God gave him a little longer to get to know and accept Him as his personal Savior. Now it was our privilege to be the ones to get him to do that.

We walked down the hospital hall with our motorcycle helmets under our arms. I could hear the patient bellowing to the nurses. Most people feared him, but he didn't scare me and I doubt he scared them, for by now they probably knew his bark was worse than his bite. His petite wife, who hardly came up to his belt buckle, could shake her finger at him and he would become a pussy cat and do whatever she wanted.

"It was no trouble finding you," I smiled as I bent over to kiss his forehead. He knew we had heard him yelling.

"Isn't this the day you head for Mexico?" he inquired, ignoring my comments.

"Yes, indeed, but we couldn't leave

without checking to see if you were in good voice. And you are, so we can go now."

"Well, I've been lying here thinking. How are you coming with the financial part of the trip?"

"Funny, you should ask," I responded.

"That's what I thought." The logger turned to his wife and said, "Write them a check, like what we talked about just before they came."

"I already did," she smiled and walked over to John and handed him the check.

"You two be on your way! You'll need to stop at a bank before you leave town. There's enough there so you two can enjoy Disneyland and eat out once in a while. Joanne will need a break from cooking so primitively."

He smiled and you could tell he was actually proud of himself. It seems that giving away one's money always warms one's heart.

"We'll see you at church when we get back, and you can look at all the pictures." I knew he would be there, as it is true, "where your money is, there will your heart be also."

Now we always pray before we leave a hospital room, but I could see John was a bit overwhelmed with the Lord's answer to our money problems as he had just peeked at the check, so he said, "Angel, will you pray for him before we go?"

When we arrived back at the church the young people, their parents, and all the church folk were gathering around for a farewell prayer before we started our trip into Mexico to work on a mission. Everyone could feel God's Spirit moving amongst us and it gave us all goose bumps. Were we really ready for this adventure that was to follow?

The bus filled with teenagers who had worked hard to get to go on this trip. (Some for the wrong reasons: a boyfriend was going, they wanted to find a boyfriend, hoping to get away from Mom and Dad for a while. But no matter why they went, I knew it would be life changing.)

The parents of one of the teenagers were following us in their van; in case the bus should break down, the van could go for help. It would later be used for emergency trips to the hospital as well. We had not even cleared the city limits when the college couple with us started leading us in songs, which was to be one of the biggest blessings on the whole trip. If you didn't know the song, not to worry, you would know it by the second or third day for sure. By the time you got home you would have trouble getting those songs out of your head.

  The Lord had certainly given us just the right couple to work with our youth! Rob had just gotten back from the war and enrolled at Northwood Christian College. He and his wife had heard John preach in chapel and decided that they would come help us harvest souls for Christ in our area. We thanked God daily for them. Rob had been a pilot and had his plane shot out from under him behind enemy lines. He ejected, and on the way down he promised God if He would take care of him then he would give his life to serving Him. One of those war-time promises—but this one was being kept. Rob's wife, Becky, was a perfect match for him; a cute, bubbly lady whom you liked immediately. The love of the Lord radiated from both of them. Rob would drive some too and relieve John. Only the highway, unlike the skies, kept making new lanes and the far right one would often exit. Rob didn't know the highway and many a time we were stuck in the wrong lane.

 Just after we exited the city limits of our town, one of the kids said, "Please stop at the next rest area!" That was just a preview of things to come. John was later to be heard saying, "I don't think we missed one rest area between here and Mexico!" Luckily we were only going to Medford that night to stay at the church Becky's folks attended. Darkness overcame us as we reached the Medford city limits. At the church a fine meal was waiting for us. It didn't take the young people long to show their appreciation. I knew there were bottomless pits to be filled on this tour!

 John gathered us all together for one of his exceptional devotionals, and then we were off to the sleeping bags that would serve as beds for the next three weeks. My personal evening prayers for the next three weeks would be ones of praise and thankfulness for the day we had all been through, my morning prayers were asking for His presence and strong guidance. He never failed. (He will not fail you either, try Him.)

After a wonderful breakfast at the church, and morning devotions, we were off once again to visit all the rest areas along I-5. I attribute everyone's getting along so well together, in spite of many not sleeping too well, to the fun songs we sang constantly, making the miles slip away. Also, those great morning, noon and night devotions.

"Tiger, I don't think the devil can possibly get a toe-hold on this trip! God's presence is so real. There is no bickering, or 'me first' attitude at all, thanks to your great devotions! You really are reaching the kids, and us adults too." I encouraged John on the third day.

It was getting dusk as we pulled into

All People's Church in Los Angeles, where John had made arrangements for our group to eat and spend the night. We all piled out of the bus and ran to the back door of the church. But—"It's locked! It's locked!" the first arrivals informed us. Sure enough, all the church doors were locked. John hunted up a phone and came back rather sad-faced.

"I can't find anyone to talk to about this. No one answers the number I have."

"Oh well, maybe we can stay a night early in San Diego."

John ran for the phone again and this time came back grinning.

We all piled back into the bus. Rob took the wheel, giving John a rest, and we were off. Rush hour traffic was upon us and the lanes kept exiting. Poor Rob was stuck in the exiting lane too many times but never did he have to actually exit.

Weary, tired and hungry, the young people dragged themselves off the bus. No one complained. Speak of miracles! The women had prepared a lovely meal for us, with lots of treats besides. Everyone got a good night's sleep and the next day we were all eager to hear the director of the Mexican mission project talk to us and orientate us for what our jobs would be.

Everyone seemed pleased with their assignments. We would be painting a school, stopping at an orphanage to help play with the darling kids there. Also, filling pot-holes in the back roads, mending fences and making new fences (digging post holes, no easy task in dry clay-like ground.)

Everett, the driver of the follow-up van, took the bus to be serviced while we were having our meeting, so that everything would be shipshape when we crossed the border into Mexico.

The next day we thanked our hosts, and headed south of the border. We traveled hours along a curvy highway next to the ocean before reaching a little town that would be our supply station for the next week. We spotted a little restaurant and John whispered sweetly to me.

"Looks like that would be a good place to take everyone to one night, as a special treat for them and you. It doesn't look like anyone would get food poisoning."

I agreed happily. I had asked all those going with us to eat at least one yogurt each day for two weeks prior to our leaving the United States. The live cultures were supposed to kill the germs that might cause intestinal trouble. We would see how well it worked. (It did!) Our first stop was at the orphanage.

Everyone hurried out of the hot bus and onto the dirt playground where children of all ages were shyly waiting for us. Each of our young people took one of the small ones to shower attention on. The little ones seemed really happy with the attention. With only one teacher and one helper available for so many little ones, individual attention was scarce. The teacher and the helper also had to prepare the meals, clean, and do the many, many necessary jobs in running the orphanage.

When we got back on the bus all of our group vowed to come back and help again. This stop had been a life-changing experience for many of them. The children clung to their new friends and it was plain to see the young people's hearts had been touched.

"When we get back to the States we must do something to earn money for them!" One of the young people informed the rest of us.

"We can clean our closets and send clothes, too," another chimed in. We had taken supplies and clothes with us and they were so gratefully received. The next time we stopped the little ones were wearing the clothes we had brought. It was very touching.

The road to turn off to the camp where we would stay was not too far from the orphanage; we would pass it going to the village each day.

"We have arrived," John announced as we pulled to a stop at the end of a rutted, pot-holed road. Everyone scrambled out of the bus and the van. There was a shed that would hold us all for meals, but it was not big enough for all of us to sleep in. I looked around. All I saw was another small shed by a woodpile about 100 yards away. Both sheds were filthy dirty. Some men in the yard were patting clay into shapes like bricks and laying them out to dry. The heat was intense so I was sure the bricks would dry nicely. None of the buildings were made of brick—so the men must have sold them.

"First order of business had better be to help me clean this building, if anyone wants supper," I uselessly shouted.

To get help cleaning was not going to be easy as some local young boys had come by and were standing shyly on the edge of the property. From somewhere our ball appeared and a game of kick ball soon began, mixing laughter and sweat together. Oh well, Hazel and I would do the best we could and clean a little space to use as the kitchen. As evening approached the men made a roaring campfire and we roasted hot dogs. The smell must have attracted the locals, as many from around the area showed up. Our young people were more than glad to share their supper with them.

After showing them how to make

"s'more's," we all settled down around the campfire.

We began to sing songs and even one or two in Spanish. The locals joined right in on the Spanish ones. John's talk that night was especially moving and he would add some words in Spanish for our new friends every now and then, too. He prayed at the end in Spanish and then in English. We said our goodnights and headed up to the shed.

John and I decided to put the boys on one side of the building and the girls on the other. The other couple, and we, would sleep in between them. "Too many hormones running around here," John explained.

We rigged up a pan with water so that each could wet a wash cloth and wash their face. Each one was also given a paper cup of water with which to brush their teeth. I was surprised there was no grumbling—just joking and laughter.

We all finally settled into our sleeping bags and then we heard this awful noise.

"What's that?" the girls whispered.

John began to laugh. One of the boys was snoring, then another took it up too. Soon it sounded like wild animals in the middle of the jungle! We all covered our ears but no one could get to sleep. What to do? We hadn't counted on this! In the churches where we slept on the way down, the girls were in a different room from the boys.

Hazel said sleepily, "I'll take the girls and go down to the woodshed to sleep."

This was not an appealing idea to me but I knew I would have to go too. With flashlights in hand we trudged down to the little shed. Each girl found a spot and once again we settled down to sleep.

Soon giggling burst out again.

"I can still hear them!" the girls giggled. "At least now it is far away enough so it won't keep us awake."

The sun coming in the cracks in the wall woke us the next morning. I gingerly sat up to stretch my sore muscles and bones. I was startled into full awakedness by a scream from Hazel directed at me. "Don't move, Joanne!" she yelled.

I opened my eyes to see in front of me the shape of a violin on the tummy of a spider that was dangling from the curl on my forehead...

"Black widow! Don't move," Hazel informed me.

Happily I was not scared of spiders. Snakes, yes; spiders, no. So I reached up and grabbed the little thread he was dangling from and dropped him to the floor. Then I had to find something to kill him with, as I couldn't step on him with my bare feet. With one hand I grabbed my shoe and BANG! He was dead.

"OK—that is a reminder that we all have to check our clothes and shoes before we put them on. Shake your socks," I told the girls.

Later that day as the fellas were getting wood by the shed they came across more deadly spiders and a couple of snakes.

"It really is not too safe to sleep down there, Angel. Let's figure out something else to do," my concerned husband cautioned me. But what else was there to do?

"You could keep those snoring people awake until we gals get to sleep, but then if anyone wakes up in the night they would never be able to get back to sleep," I offered my not too helpful suggestion.

We finally decided that my suggestion was our best bet and so that night we all slept up in the main shed. Those who woke up in the night were doomed to a snoring concert.

After breakfast and devotions we all chose our chores and got busy with happy hearts. All knew they were needed and that is such a neat feeling! Again, in spite of lack of water, lots of heat, dust, and fatigue there was no complaining. *God is surely blessing our mission,* I thought.

By noon the sun was blazing down. We all found shade under which to eat our lunch. A report was given on the progress of the projects. The schoolhouse painting was going fine. You could really see the difference. But the crew told a sad tale about the enormous amount of bird droppings on the school house floor. They knew they needed to sweep it up, they said, but no one could stay in there for any length of time without getting sick and vomiting. Several of them tried it without success. We all knew only our farm boy, our preacher man, John, could save the day.

The pot-holes were filling up. That was really back-breaking work, but some of the girls pitched right in and did their share.

The boys had to dig the post holes for the fence as the ground was just too hard, but that too was going well. They filled the holes with some of our precious water and in the morning they were soft enough to dig.

Hazel and I decided it was time for us to go into the little village and get more water and supplies. We would take Everett with us as we would need help to get the bottled water into the van. So, after setting the homemade rolls to rise (I found it not any harder to cook for one hundred than for ten; you just use more flour) we hopped in the van and headed to the little town.

"The heat is stifling," Hazel commented as we all wiped our brows for the umpteenth time.

We soon found a *tienda* (store) and were busy purchasing the things on our list. I was careful not to buy any produce that could not be treated sufficiently so no one would get sick. We soaked lettuce in iodine to kill the unwanted germs, but first we had to treat the water we soaked it in. We boiled all our water as it cost too much to used bottled water for everything.

Weary and extremely hot, we pulled into camp just in time to start supper. Everyone was hungry and barely walking, their seldom used muscles aching. My baked bread was a big hit. Years later many of the young people would tell me that one of the highlights of the trip was my homemade bread.

We all welcomed the campfire that night outside where a breeze helped cool us off, and songs lifted our spirits. After John's message three of the young people announced they wanted to accept Christ into their lives and be baptized.

"We will have a baptismal service tomorrow in the ocean," John announced. Everyone was so tired even the loud snoring did not keep us awake.

The next day found everyone excited about the ocean baptism. After breakfast we all piled in the bus and headed for the beach. We sang songs on the way and after arriving.

"Everyone please form a circle around our baptismal candidates," John instructed us in the firm but kind voice that we had all come to respect. Out into the water we trotted until we were waist high. There weren't any waves, which made it very pleasant. A circle was formed around the three young people and we all held hands. One of the adults stayed back and took pictures to show the church members back home. Each person took their turn being put under the water in the name of the Father, the Son, and the Holy Spirit. It was a very meaningful experience for all.

"This might be an appropriate time to all go to town and eat supper out tonight. You could use a break, Angel," John shared his thoughts with me on the way back to camp.

"You won't get any objection from me, Tiger," I smiled. That freed me up to help paint on the schoolhouse too.

Everyone sponge bathed and cleaned themselves the best way possible that evening and we headed into the little village to see if we could find the restaurant we had spotted on the way down.

"There it is!" several shouted at once. It would not be easy parking the bus on the narrow streets, but John did the best he could and we all rushed out and into the restaurant, anticipating air conditioning, but that was too much to hope for. A big overhead fan would have to do.

"Everyone has to drink pop. No water, please!" I warned everybody.

The food was not that expensive so we didn't have to put restrictions on anyone's choices. Everyone on this tour was very pleased with his or her meal. It turned out to be a very pleasant memory for everyone.

"I can hardly wait to share with our friends who donated the generous check how pleasant a memory they allowed us all to reap," I shared on the bus back to camp.

The next day, as I was washing my face, one of the girls came up to me and excitedly proclaimed, "Mrs. King! Gale hit her head and we think she has a concussion. She is really sick!"

I rushed over to where Gale was lying on her sleeping bag. One look told me she needed professional medical help, more than what we could get for her here. After consulting with the others it was decided that I would drive her back to the States to the San Diego hospital, which would be a scary, lonesome, and a bit dangerous road to take. A lot of prayers would have to get us through.

"No flat tires or car trouble out in the middle of nowhere, Lord, please," I pleaded with God. "I know *you* can handle it, but I'm not sure *I* can," I reminded Him.

As Gale was so sick, she didn't feel like talking much. This made the trip a bit long but we finally pulled into the emergency driveway at the Clairmont hospital. Gale was diagnosed, medicine given, and we were back on the road to camp. She did have a concussion!

"I think we can make it back by dark, honey," I smiled. Sure enough, we pulled into camp, none the worse for wear just before total darkness overtook us.

"I hope that is the last trip to the hospital we have to take with this group," I confided to John that night. And it was.

Soon—way too soon—our time in Mexico was coming to a close. Everyone who had come on this trip was changed for the better. We all discovered things about ourselves that were good. It turned out we could handle bad situations much better than we thought, and some were surprised to find that they could find joy in helping others. The young people had found out that they were OK, and didn't have the strong need anymore for someone else to tell them in order for them to feel good about themselves. God had confirmed that to them from the inside out. They found out who they were, and they liked who they found.

After saying our tearful good-byes to

the orphanage children and their helpers, (I noticed many tears in all our eyes, including the boys and girls alike) we were off for the United States. The discussion on the bus was all about the darling orphanage children and how each one of us would have liked to have taken one of them home with us.

We were able to stay again in the San Diego church, and from there we enjoyed a day at Disneyland.

On the way home, things were no different than on the way down. Again, we stopped at every rest area between Mexico and Springfield, Oregon, missing not a one. On our next family outing, John commented as we passed a rest area. "Oh, it's so nice to breeze right by and not have to stop!"

As we pulled into the church parking lot the parents of the young people were eagerly waiting for their kids. After a prayer of thanksgiving we too headed for home and our own shower and little bed. How nice . . .

12
After Mexico—Troubles

John was asked to direct a church camp for high school kids up in the mountains the next summer. He was very good at this and had a great group of counselors. I didn't go in order to stay home with Mike and Tom. The camp was only two hours away, so I was not too surprised at midnight the first night when I heard the front door open. There stood John, looking kinda sheepish.

"May I sleep with you?" he grinned. I knew he would have to get up by four A.M. to get back to camp as the campers would be waking up. Nevertheless, John appeared each and every night at midnight. I was hoping he was able to take a nap. Several accepted Christ at church camp so that made all the effort and hard work worth it.

After the first year at the church we began to plan our family vacation, which would have to be squeezed in between weddings, funerals, and Vacation Bible School. "I'll have to ask for time off work, too." I reminded the family. Then we found out the boys had track events during the summer. It looked impossible. We decided to schedule a date anyway and see what happened. It worked. I began by making reservations at Yellowstone Park. No one suspected this would be our last vacation as a family. Looking back on our time together we all agree we wouldn't have done anything any differently.

One of our young people offered to come over and feed Scottie for us; our nice neighbors said they would keep a close eye on our place. We packed the car and were off.

"Yellowstone is such a fun place to vacation with the kids," I whispered to John that night. We had rented a very nice tent house. The bathroom was outside, and at night it wasn't great fun—but other than that I felt perfectly safe and slept well.

"Remember the last time we were in a tent house?" John asked me.

"Oh, yes. It was at Yosemite and you built a bonfire and put the diapers in a boiling pot. You stood on two logs and used a long tree branch to stir them. They came out fine, too."

Each day John called back to the church to see if all was OK. But one day I heard him say "Oh, no!" and I knew our vacation was up. He turned from the phone and explained, "Scottie has bitten the little sister of the young person who is feeding him! She had to have stitches. He bit her on the nose and mouth."

It was so hard to believe that our beloved Scottie would bite anyone. We knew we had to go home and take care of the matter. We no sooner pulled into the driveway when our neighbor came running over.

"Don't kill the dog, it wasn't his fault! The child got her face in the dog's dish and ate his food. Scottie growled at her so loud we heard him from over here. I came and yelled at her to get her face out of his feeding bowl, but she just laughed and tried to eat some more. Scottie snapped at her but she still wouldn't leave him alone. The older sister was inside getting water and didn't take the child's face out of Scottie's bowl. It wasn't his fault. He doesn't deserve to die!"

John went over to the family's house and saw the little girl, whose face did look awful. He offered to pay for the doctor and any care she would need. He assured the family that we would get rid of the dog.

"Her face does look bad, Angel," he reported to me. "I hope it doesn't leave any permanent scars or that she has to have plastic surgery."

We explained to the boys that we had to get rid of our beloved Scottie but that we would see if we could find a nice home for him in the country. And this is just what happened. We missed Scottie so much, but he was happy running free on a nice farm.

Meanwhile, life would have to go on without Scottie. The church was doing nicely; John's stature in the community was growing and so was the church. He soon found himself on way too many interdenominational committees; it seemed like every night was being taken up. I was aware of the influence he was having when he asked the Bible Study class, "What would you do if the police told you, 'You must deny Christ or die'?" Everyone tried to reason it out: like, "If I lived I could witness for Him longer." But then one of the ladies said, "I know exactly what I would do. I'd look and see what preacher John was doing, then I'd be brave enough to do the same." We all knew what John would do.

Michael, our youngest boy, took after his Dutch and Scandinavian ancestors in his body build and his strength. By the sixth grade he was a big, strong, handsome blond lad. His size, combined with his good nature, made him a target for jealous school bullies. He was often picked on, but his father had instructed him not to fight back. So Mickey would walk off with one or two boys hanging on his back and he trying to shake them off.

Where the playground teacher was, I do not know—but one day Mickey came home from school bloody and bruised. John had had enough. In spite of the pleas from Mickey, John went to school the next day and spoke with the principal.

"I want you to know that I have given Mickey permission to defend himself on the playground, as your playground teachers are not supervising adequately," he explained.

The very next day we got a call to "please come to school and speak with the principal." Off John went immediately.

There had been a fight, and with pushing and shoving some boys got skinned up and hurt. Mike had warned them his daddy had told him he could fight back.

John refreshed the principal's memory on what he had said the day before. It was left at that; no more fights were ever called to our attention again.

It was so nice to have a husband to settle these matters.

Whatever would I do without him? I wondered. Sadly, I was to soon find out.

13
"Till Death Do Us Part"

"Here's a letter for you, Mrs. King," John announced one noon as he swung in the front door. "Special delivery. I'm delivering it to you."

He handed me the business-size envelope and I glanced at the return address.

"Hummmmm, this is from the city of Springfield."

I tore the envelope open and my heart sank. A big lump came in my throat. In my mind I was once again standing before the doctor in South America and hearing those unwelcome words ring in my ears.

"Your husband has maybe less than a year to live. His cholesterol is so high. The heart attack he had has done some damage but the thing to fear is another heart attack. I am sure he will not see his fortieth birthday." That was seven years ago.

I slowly began to read the letter. It seemed that the city, together with the Ministerial Association, was sponsoring a city-wide seminar on "Death and Dying." They were going to have a panel of speakers and then those attending could ask questions. On the panel would be a priest, a bishop, a rabbi, and myself, if I would accept the invitation.

Just thinking about it made my heart race, my breathing come fast, and a sinking pit in my stomach. This hit too close to home. Could I handle this?

"You'll do great, Angel! Why don't you do it? Maybe it's the Lord helping you to prepare for the future?"

"Easy for you to say! I'll be the one left, and you'll be the one going to heaven," I snapped back. However, I knew there was probably truth in what he was saying.

Therefore I did accept and started to work on my thoughts about death and dying. I'd tell them about death in South America and that awful funeral wagon going all over town playing *Silent Night*. I'd include how in some areas when the man died they would throw the wife and children in the grave, too, and bury them all together. That way they would not be a burden to the community.

Finally I had to come face to face with my thoughts on death. I began to relax and see God's overall plan for mankind. I was happy with the thoughts God had put into my head. I was ready for the seminar.

The specified evening came and John and I slipped into the downtown meeting hall a little early. We watched the people stream in.

"It seems that this is a very important topic for a lot of people," John whispered in my ear. Before I could answer they were escorting me up to the platform and sat me on the end of the panel next to the Catholic priest.

This means I will either be first or last, I imagine, I reasoned with myself. Sure enough, I was introduced first and asked to speak first. The audience was not to ask questions until the last speaker had given his talk.

At least they won't be bored yet, as I am

the first and they will pay attention to what I have to say, I encouraged myself. Sure enough, the audience seemed to hang on every word.

This truly must be from God, I thought. I knew it was from God because I had gleaned all the scriptures on death I could find in the Bible.

Encouraged by the response to my words, the second speaker began to talk. Soon all of us had spoken and it was time for questions. First came a question from a physician, then one from an attorney; a mailman was next.

"It has become clear to me that death is certainly a leveler of class, education and prestige. No one escapes. It is just a matter of time," I shared with John later.

The time slipped by very fast and I had learned a lot. I would go home and record the thoughts in my journal. They would prove very helpful in the near future.

When we arrived home I felt like I had run a marathon! Every muscle ached, and I was tired beyond belief.

"How can mental strain wear you out so much?" I inquired. As John used his brain every day, all day, he was ready with the facts and figures on how it can be physically draining, but I fell asleep before I heard everything.

John came home the next day from his hospital calls and announced, "I think I was sicker than the ones I went to visit today. I would have liked to have traded places with them. Angel, the time has come, I feel, that I need to resign from some of the committees that I am on. Would you drive me around to the meetings and give me support?"

And so it was evening after evening I drove John around town to the various committees he was on and he resigned from them, one by one.

"I didn't realize you had gotten yourself into so many commitments. I'm sure glad you are resigning from them."

"This resigning business is hard. You have to give a good reason and it is embarrassing for me," John complained as he crawled into the car after he had resigned from his last committee.

It seemed his health was declining each day. We would go to the mall to walk and he would just go from one bench to the next one, huffing and puffing all the way. He was sweating and it was just spring, not hot weather at all.

John's doctor had refused to renew his cholesterol medicine, saying that his cholesterol was fine now, down to that of a newborn babe. I am convinced that it began to climb and no one detected it. One man in the area had by-pass surgery, but died soon afterward, so John said, "No use going through that! Someday they will perfect it but I probably won't be around to see it." How prophetic he was.

The night after John had resigned from his last committee obligation, I was sitting on his lap and we were laughing and having fun when he said, "Let's go to bed." I hopped up and we went arm in arm down the hall to the bedroom. The boys were asleep; it was dark outside and inside the room. As I put my head on the pillow a long shaft of light appeared in the corner of the room. It went from the floor to the ceiling. I got goose bumps. I was frightened.

"What is that?" I spoke reverently into John's ear. "I'm scared!"

I got up and checked to see if a stream of light could possibly be coming through the curtains, or door, or *anywhere*. Finding not a clue I jumped into bed, but I was shaking.

John held me and calmly said, "Angel, we can fly to the moon but we don't know much about the supernatural. That light is a friendly Spirit. I am in such pain, the Lord has said I could go now but you will not release me. He has promised to help you raise the boys. Please release me! I have participated in many a healing here on this earth but as I ask God for my own healing He tells me no."

Everything within me screamed "NO!" But I could see that the pain he was in was excruciating. I knew Heaven would be a wonderful place for John: no pain, just everlasting joy with Jesus, his true friend. How selfish of me to refuse John's request.

The light in the corner was still very brilliant and glowing.

"Lord," I prayed, "must I give up this man? He is a part of me, yet I must bow to Your will. In this case, You certainly know my wishes."

The next morning I expected to find John dead—but he wasn't. I felt maybe it was just a bad dream—but I knew it wasn't when John awoke and said, "Thank you Angel, for releasing me." *How did John know?*

"I know I will be scared to go to bed tonight for fear that bright light might come again," I confided in him.

"Don't worry! It will not be here tonight." John reassured me. I wondered how he could be so sure, but I had kids to get off to school so I put it out of my mind.

John dressed and went to work but came home early. He decided to go out with the boys when they got home from school. I waved as they jogged off around the block.

With a smile on my face I started supper. Then I heard the boys coming back.

"Mom, help! Mom!" They were dragging John; they bought him in and he fell to the floor. I called 911.

John kept saying "I can't breathe, I can't breathe!"

We propped him up against the davenport. Then the oldest boy started giving him CPR. The 911 people came and they took over.

A neighbor came and offered to ride with me to the hospital as I would not be allowed to go in the ambulance.

"I'll be fine," I assured her. How nice that she didn't listen to me but came anyway.

Another neighbor came and started finishing up cooking our supper, and sat the boys down to feed them.

At the hospital we had barely sat down when an emergency doctor came out and asked me to go into a little room with him.

"The 911 people said your son kept your husband's vital signs going but John was dead when they arrived at your house.

They could not revive him. I am so sorry. Where do you want us to send the body?"

I wanted to scream "That 'body' was my husband!"

No matter how long ahead of time you know someone is going to die, when the time comes it is still not expected. It comes as a shock.

As John and I had often talked about our deaths and funerals I knew just where he wanted to go; I knew just what he wanted and when. I knew what songs he wanted, what poems—everything. The only thing I did differently was to let him lie in state at the funeral parlor for loved ones to come see him and say their last good-bye.

I was glad my neighbor had come with me but I assured her I was fine to drive home. Actually I only *thought* I was fine. I was in a daze and numbness had set in to buffer the shock.

When I got home the task of telling the boys was facing me. John's voice rang in my ears, "God has promised to help you raise our boys. Do not be afraid."

I thanked the neighbors and sent them home. They admonished me to be sure and eat "to keep my strength up." They did not realize that a lump had come into my throat that would not allow food to pass through, not even liquids. I could not take pills even though the doctor had left me some to relax me so I could sleep. I didn't need them anyway. God cradled me in His arms and I slept like a baby. I was thin then but by the time the lump went away I was skinny.

The boys and I gathered in the front room and I told them their earthly father was gone, so now their heavenly Father would become to them like their earthly Father. Furthermore, I wanted them to know that no matter what people said, Tim (our oldest) was not the "head of the household," nor was he "the man of the house now." No way! God was the head of our house; my protector and shield and theirs, too.

We had some practical matters to take

care of. The boys decided they would go to school the next day to be a witness to show everyone how Christians face death. They did, and indeed it was a witness, as one of their teachers started coming to church as a result, he said.

Many phone calls had to be made. The first one went to my parents who were vacationing in California. They dropped everything and came to Oregon as fast as possible. I called my boss and told him I would not be in the next day. The next day happened to be his birthday and I had made and decorated a cake, so I snuck it in before work and left it on his desk.

I called the gal I worked with and she was there almost before I hung up. My boss and his wife came shortly thereafter. I called my sister, who flew up from Sacramento the next day. I met her at the airport and knew I had some back-up.

The fellows at the funeral parlor were all good friends of John. They asked to help with the service at no charge to me, "As our gift to John," they said. What help that was! Especially since John had died at the beginning of the week and he had wanted his service to be during the regular Sunday worship service so he would have to be kept for several days. This was a double blessing as John's families were coming from Idaho and wanted to say their good-byes to him too.

 Everyone gave me advice. They were crying and crying, but no tears came to my eyes and I wondered why everyone was crying. People said, "How strong you are!" No, I wasn't strong, I was numb and it just had not sunk into my consciousness yet. I was not traveling in reality. I feel this is nature's anesthesia for a person whose heart has just been ripped out. The pain has to come slowly—or we could not bear it.

 The house was constantly full of company. I put out my handmade blanket on the davenport. I had spent years weaving it and it was so pretty. After the funeral when the last of John's relatives left I looked for my blanket and it was missing. As John's mother used to make blankets, too, I thought maybe one of the relatives thought it was hers and took it by mistake. I called them all but all denied even seeing it. I was sad to lose it. I would never be able to make another one.

Kind friends told me to get all the money out of the checking account as soon as possible because the bank would freeze the account. I did as they suggested but could not believe the bank would do that. But they did!!

The day of the funeral came and we were picked up by the funeral parlor's car. The rest of the staff were at the church helping to park the cars. That was helpful as it seemed the whole town was turning out. I was grateful I had a reserved seat with my family. The church secretary had prepared a booklet with the tributes people wanted to say about John. I have included some of them in the back of this book.

The church service was a praise to God and to His servant John. It was a celebration of John's life. The choir sang his favorite anthem, "God Gave the Song." The words were so meaningful. I was deeply moved by the whole service—but still no tears came.

After the service we went home and the house was full of food. Everyone was talking in hushed tones and eating. I thought, *What is wrong with them?* I would hold them when they cried but I would not cry. That would come later. When the tears did start it seemed they would never stop.

Like Thomas Dorsey, who wrote the hymn "Precious Lord, Take My Hand," I can say, "God has healed my spirit." I too have learned that when we are in our deepest grief, when we feel farthest from God, this is when He is closest. We are then more open to His restoring power. So I will go on living for God, willingly and joyfully, until that day comes when He will take me and gently lead me home.

My scripture for the coming days would be Psalms 18:32. "He fills me with strength and protects me wherever I go."

The song that I would sing each day going to work was "Because He lives, I can face tomorrow; because He lives, all fear is gone. I know Who holds the future, and life is worth the living, just because He lives." By the time I would reach work tears were streaming down my face. This release was blessed assurance. I would be blowing my nose. What a beautiful sight I must have made.

The day after the funeral I was back at work but nothing was the same ever again.

The following is taken from the little booklet put together by the church secretary from writings various people gave to her.

In Memoriam of John D. King

November 21,
1932–March 18, 1975

The deepest impression that John King made in my life was the way in which he became a servant of God. It was always John's wish to follow the will of God. He had the choice and he chose God's will. John, through his ministry to Northwood Christian Church, committed his every task to the hands of Jesus. The communication that took place between him and God moved mountains to the glory of this church.

Dick Meyers

Thank you, Lord, for bringing John King to Northwood. Thank you for the life he lived here in Springfield, teaching us to love one another and to forgive each other. He tried to make us aware of Your presence each moment of the day and to trust You for our needs.
 Lord, may Your work be carried on here with greater zeal because we know that your Spirit lived in his life and now lives in ours. Bless his family and care for them.
 In the name of Jesus we thank you.

Doris McCord

I was lying in a hospital bed when I first met John King. I faced four hours of surgery in the morning. We talked some and then John asked permission to pray for me.
 Two years later I came to his church.

Within two Sundays I knew I had missed out on something beautiful. I am sorry.

Nine short Sundays, but oh how great for me. John will live in my heart because through him I have come to know Jesus for the first time.

Thank you, Lord, for John King.

>Jim Lacock

John was more than a minister, he was a friend. He was always there when I needed him.

His love for Jesus radiated all the time. He loved us and showed us how to love.

I was privileged to work with him the last few months as his secretary. Each time I saw him he had a warm smile and a kind word that made my day a little brighter because I felt the love of God.

Thank you, Lord, for John King. Thank you for the privilege of knowing him. I will never forget John.

>Judy Lacock

John shored me up. He was so very much there when I needed him. He lessened my fear of death, helped me find the strength I needed so that I could face that which was necessary, knowing that I would win either way. Somewhere in the middle of the turmoil of my next crisis I suspect I will still hear John's voice reminding me to put my faith and acceptance of God's will into the hands of Jesus.

The sunshine of God's smile will be with me the rest of my life.

Thank you, Joanne, for a yellow coat. (John often wore a bright yellow sport coat.)

Mary Bruce

It seems but a short time ago that we received a letter from Jerry Nelson, interim minister at Northwood, beginning:

"Good news, John King has accepted our call to become pastor of Northwood."

He should be here July 1, 1972. Then the sad evening Dick Meyers called to tell us John King had passed away, March 18, 1975.

Our knowing John was but a short 32 months. We grew to love him and be strengthened by his Sunday sermons. No, not only on Sunday was one strengthened by John's beliefs, but any time you were around him. He lived his religion. He didn't have to push it off on people, for as they saw him they too wanted to possess the peace, love, happiness, tolerance, and compassion that he reflected.

His humor and quick wit were to be envied. They were ever present, and were even appreciated when you were the object of the "quip." Oh, his way of dress—my, how we appreciated it. We thought at first "he is wild!" But we soon realized "that is John, bright and cheerful."

He shall remain in our memory forever. We will always recall something or someplace where John had a mark on our life. Northwood grew because of him.

We thank God for having known such a man as John. May his strength be our strength now. With the God he loved he now rests in peace.

Emerick and Gladys
Hultin

John King and his family were an answer to prayer in their coming to Northwood Christian Church. The first time I heard him speak it was like beautiful rain drops falling on a dried-up sponge. I soaked up every drop that I could.

The words he spoke of Jesus always brought a renewal and strengthening of my spirit. What a thrill, what joy and peace of mind to be able to laugh and make a joyful noise unto the Lord!

I loved to hear John tell about Northwood being an answer to his and his family's prayers, and to hear about his love affair with Northwood. I knew it was a two-way affair. Once he said, "I keep wondering how long the honeymoon will last?" But I don't believe it ever ended. It just kept right on growing and growing.

I saw so many prayers answered that at times my heart would be filled to bursting. I would want to say, "Lord, I don't know if I can take any more joy," but sure enough another prayer would be answered and once again I would rejoice.

John helped us to grow in love. I never dreamt in my wildest dream that one church could love another so much. To be able to go to a friend and tell them, "I love you," and to know that they love you too—what a blessing! He taught us all how to love. Not by saying, "Do it this way or that way," but by his loving each and every one of us. We felt and knew Christ's love for all of us.

He isn't with us anymore and we are sorrowed by that fact. But in the few short years he was with us I saw more happen than I had in dozens of churches in different parts of the United States, thus far in my lifetime.

I thank God and I praise His Name for sending John to us when we needed him most. I praise God for giving us the strength to go on in the Lord's work, as that will be proof that John led and taught his flock well. What greater memorial to God than what has happened at Northwood.

I also believe that now will be a time of testing of our strength and love as we prepare to go through the process of choosing a new minister. This I know can be done, as we all have constant prayers for each other and the whole body of Christ at Northwood. God will answer our prayers by sending us another "spirit filled" minister to guide us.

Thank you, Jesus.

Rosann Stewart

When one attempts to describe the impressions of a man, it is somewhat like trying to convey to another's senses the taste of a peach; almost impossible.

John King impressed me in many ways. At first I sensed a man with many gifts, one who could supply a need—leadership with a flair. Yes, but more. A spirituality housed in human form with traits easily related to.

Away from the pulpit, a quiet, sensitive man with a great love for his people, always aware of their needs. A gentleness with an ever present smile—a purpose with patience for others to see. John was easy to talk with—a good listener, full of good humor—a punster of the first order.

In the pulpit he spoke with authority and assurance. His message somehow always seemed to address the needs and concerns that were uppermost in our thoughts. He was an exciting speaker. No one ever left morning service half asleep, but always with a clearer understanding of God's plan for our lives and certain of His love.

John was a new experience for me because he believed in miracles, the baptism of the Holy Spirit and speaking in tongues. He had personally experienced all three. I have often wondered in the past of the success of our Pentecostal brothers. Their parking lot is crammed for any kind of service, even on a work night, while we seemed to be struggling. But now our parking lot is full and our sanctuary is filled regularly. I credit John King for this transformation, because, Praise

God, he taught us to love. To love ourselves, because we know God loves us just as we are, because we are saved because Jesus Christ died—just for us—and for others because they are brothers and sisters in Christ. As a result we are more dedicated, more committed, more concerned, and new people are joining us in our worship because they find here an answer to their needs. John King has shown us a miracle.

I'm sure we won't forget John. When I learned he was gone I wondered how we were going to get along without him. However, I know we will do well, as he has helped to prepare us. He has set a goal for us and has made us more aware of our mission, both individually and as a congregation, as this part of the body of Christ. We aren't going to let him down.

Northwood has a road map—God designed it, Christ made it available to everyone, and here at Northwood John has hung it in front of us and even put up the signs pointing the way.

We thank God for John King and his family.

Dick Meyers

John King has been with us now long enough that we will never forget him. He has given so much to each of us individually and as a group. His life was successful because he let Christ rule and make the decisions (something we all need to learn). Also his earthly life was built on a rock in the form of Joanne and the three Johns. Every successful man has a loving wife and family with him in all things. I can close my eyes and see and hear John make a comment, sometimes serious, sometimes funny, about his beautiful wife, right during the sermon. He would then look down into her smiling face with love that only a man has for his wife. The three Johns are all examples of John and Joanne's Christian love and discipline. The three boys are always smiling and friendly and a joy to be around.

Tim is no longer a boy. He is a man and will be such comfort to his mother, both in helping with the family responsibility and in showing others the love and lessons learned from his father. All are so much like John, but the most obvious resemblance to me is in Tom. He walks like John, is soft spoken like John, and is really a big ham if given an audience.—Of course, Mickey (or Mike, as he likes to be called), is fair, more like Joanne but has the best qualities of both parents.

Yes, as long as there is one of these four Kings, we will have a part of John.

We loved John and rejoice that he is now with his Father in heaven. I can hear the Lord say, "Well done, John!" We also give thanks for his family. They have been such strong examples to us this last week. If they can give thanks and carry on, surely we can do the same.

Juanita Myers

From the very beginning of our acquaintance with John, he was always so friendly and loving that he always seemed like a dear friend, as well as our pastor. His love and concern for others was reflected in everything he did. His sense of humor can be described only as "John King's," and was a constant source of delight. John's love for others must certainly have been second only to his love of the Lord, Whose will he always sought to do and Whose Spirit overflowed in him.

It will never be possible for us to read Philippians 4:13,[*] without remembering

---

[*] Philippians 4:13 "For I can do everything that God asks me to with the help of Christ who gives me the strength and power."

John and how he claimed that promise for himself and shared it with others.

We rest in the assurance that the Lord has greeted John with, "Well done, good and faithful servant."

Ron and Becky Blakely

A Poem to John King
By Leone Miller

I open the Bible to pages filled with God's
    undying love
And I think of John
He had a love for people few of us attain
I read the Bible and find a new freshness
    every time I read it
And I think of John
Whose friendship was something that never
    grew old.

I find the Holy Spirit leading me into new
    insights as I search the Holy Word
And I think of John
Who had such insight into people and their
    problems.

Because he loved, he was loved in return.
Because he cared about his church, the people grew in new walks with their Lord.
Because he knew God, others came to love their Father in fresh new ways.

John King was a man of God
Whose very presence touched the lives of others
And made them strong.